John
with best
wishes & thanks

William

Past Masters
General Editor Keith Thomas

Mill

D0533754

Past Masters

AQUINAS Anthony Kenny
ARISTOTLE Jonathan Barnes
BACH Denis Arnold
FRANCIS BACON Anthony Quinton
BAYLE Elisabeth Labrousse
BERGSON Leszek Kolakowski
BERKELEY J. O. Urmson
THE BUDDHA Michael Carrithers
BURKE C. B. Macpherson
CARLYLE A. L. Le Quesne
CERVANTES P. E. Russell
CHAUCER George Kane
CLAUSEWITZ Michael Howard
COBBETT Raymond Williams
COLERIDGE Richard Holmes
CONFUCIUS Raymond Dawson
DANTE George Holmes
DARWIN Jonathan Howard
DIDEROT Peter France
GEORGE ELIOT Rosemary Ashton
ENGELS Terrell Carver
GALILEO Stillman Drake
GIBBON J. W. Burrow
GOETHE T. J. Reed
HEGEL Peter Singer

HOMER Jasper Griffin
HUME A. J. Ayer
JESUS Humphrey Carpenter
KANT Roger Scruton
LAMARCK L. J. Jordanova
LEIBNIZ G. MacDonald Ross
LOCKE John Dunn
MACHIAVELLI Quentin Skinner
MARX Peter Singer
MENDEL Vitezslav Orel
MILL William Thomas
MONTAIGNE Peter Burke
THOMAS MORE Anthony Kenny
WILLIAM MORRIS Peter Stansky
MUHAMMAD Michael Cook
NEWMAN Owen Chadwick
PASCAL Alban Krailsheimer
PETRARCH Nicholas Mann
PLATO R. M. Hare
PROUST Derwent May
RUSKIN George P. Landow
ADAM SMITH D. D. Raphael
TOLSTOY Henry Gifford
VICO Peter Burke
WYCLIF Anthony Kenny

Forthcoming

AUGUSTINE Henry Chadwick
BAGEHOT Colin Matthew
BENTHAM John Dinwiddy
JOSEPH BUTLER R. G. Frey
COPERNICUS Owen Gingerich
DESCARTES Tom Sorell
DISRAELI John Vincent
ERASMUS John McConica
GODWIN Alan Ryan
HERZEN Aileen Kelly
JEFFERSON Jack P. Greene
JOHNSON Pat Rogers
KIERKEGAARD Patrick Gardiner
LEONARDO E. H. Gombrich

LINNAEUS W. T. Stearn
MALTHUS Donald Winch
MONTESQUIEU Judith Shklar
NEWTON P. M. Rattansi
ROUSSEAU Robert Wokler
RUSSELL John G. Slater
SHAKESPEARE Germaine Greer
SOCRATES Bernard Williams
SPINOZA Roger Scruton
TOCQUEVILLE Larry Siedentop
VIRGIL Jasper Griffin

and others

William Thomas

Mill

Oxford   New York
OXFORD UNIVERSITY PRESS
1985

Oxford University Press, Walton Street, Oxford OX2 6DP

Oxford New York Toronto
Delhi Bombay Calcutta Madras Karachi
Kuala Lumpur Singapore Hong Kong Tokyo
Nairobi Dar es Salaam Cape Town
Melbourne Auckland

and associated companies in
Beirut Berlin Ibadan Mexico City Nicosia

Oxford is a trade mark of Oxford University Press

First published 1985 as an Oxford University Press paperback
and simultaneously in a hardback edition

British Library Cataloguing in Publication Data

Thomas, William, 1936–
J. S. Mill—(Past masters)
1. Mill, John Stuart   2. Philosophy—England
—Biography
I. Title   II. Series
192   B1606

ISBN 0–19–287521–3
ISBN 0–19–287520–5 Pbk

Library of Congress Cataloging in Publication Data

Thomas, William, 1936–
J. S. Mill.
(Past masters)
Bibliography: p.   Includes index.
1. Mill, John Stuart, 1806–1873.   2. Philosophers—
England—Biography.   I. Title.   II. Series,
B1606.T48   1985   192[B]   85–10639

ISBN 0–19–287521–3
ISBN 0–19–287520–5 (pbk.)

Set by Grove Graphics
Printed in Great Britain by
Cox & Wyman Ltd.
Reading, Berks

Preface

Mill's work is so widely read and has become the subject of such a vast literature that no book about him as short as this one can hope to be more than an interpretive essay. Most such books on Mill are by professional philosophers. This one is by a historian. I am of course heavily indebted to many recent critics, and cannot claim to have said anything on the following pages that has not been said by someone before me. My only claim to novelty is that I have taken seriously what Mill himself said about his education. When asked to give a short résumé of his life for a biographical dictionary he said he had been educated wholly by his father. If that is true (and it at least represents what he felt to be true at the close of his life) then a balanced assessment of Mill as a 'Past Master' must pay more attention to the formative influences on him than is usually paid. If this seems to diminish his originality in comparison with other thinkers, that may only be because other thinkers seldom state their debts so fully and so modestly. It certainly does not diminish his stature as a human being.

Many friends have helped me with this book. John Robson, Terence Ball, and Julia Annas read the manuscript and made many helpful suggestions. Alan Ryan's two books on Mill have been my constant aids, and he has cleared up a lot of my perplexities in discussion. I have learned a lot from colleagues who may not have realized what it was they were clarifying, especially Peter Pulzer, Colin Matthew, John Davis, Lucy Newlyn, and Ian Harris. Without the editorial labours of John Robson and his fellow editors in the *Collected Works*, no interpretation of Mill, least of all a historical one, can hope to avoid blunders, and

Preface

those volumes have been really invaluable. I should like to thank my wife for compiling the index. Finally, I am most grateful to Keith Thomas for inviting me to contribute to the series and for being so patient with my delays.

Oxford WILLIAM THOMAS
February 1985

Contents

Abbreviations

The following abbreviations are used in references to Mill's works:

E   J. S. Mill, *Three Essays: On Liberty, Representative Government, The Subjection of Women* (Oxford, 1912; reprinted as an Oxford University Press paperback 1978, with pagination unchanged)

W   J. M. Robson *et al.* (eds), *Collected Works of John Stuart Mill* (Toronto and London, 1963–   ). References are to volume and page. Where a number of references to the same volume appear close together in the text the reference is given in full only in the first instance; page numbers only are given thereafter.

1 Upbringing and education

John Stuart Mill was born in London in 1806. His father, James Mill, was a Scot of humble origin who, like many of his talented countrymen, had come south to earn his living as a writer. After trying journalism he decided to make a bid for fame and fortune by writing a *History of British India*. He hoped to finish it in three years, but it took eleven, and they were years of hardship, in which he had to provide for a wife and a growing family.

James Mill's work on India had a twofold significance for his son. It dominated his childhood, and it determined his career. In the Mill household everything revolved round the breadwinner and had to be subordinated to his requirements. John Mill took all his lessons from his father. He read the books his father was reading and shared the problems they raised. When he was eleven, he helped read the proofs of the *History of British India*. Soon after its publication in 1818, James Mill was appointed Assistant Examiner at the East India House, an appointment which was a tribute to his expert knowledge and a solution to his financial problems. He could now write on the philosophical and political problems which interested him. He could buy a house in the country. He could consider a liberal profession for his eldest son. For a time he thought of the law. But in 1823 there was a vacancy for another Assistant Examiner and James Mill obtained the post for his son. From then on until his retirement in 1858 John Mill served the British government of India. So while the dominant book of his boyhood was the history of the conquest of a supposedly

1

backward people, his manhood's occupation was their administration. Between them they account for that preoccupation with backward and progressive social states which marks all his political writing and much of his thinking.

The most notable fact about John Mill's education was that it was an isolating experience. This was due less to his father's poverty than his pride. James Mill had to be frugal, but he was never insolvent, and he had wealthy friends like the stockbroker economist David Ricardo and the philosopher Jeremy Bentham. John was born in the London suburbs of Pentonville, but James Mill's friendship with Bentham brought him into the centre of the city, and for a time they lived next to the old philosopher in Queen Square Place, Westminster. Between 1814 and 1819 Bentham chose to pass his summers at Ford Abbey in Somerset, and the Mills accompanied him. John Mill was later to feel grateful that he had experienced life in a medieval setting 'so unlike the mean and cramped externals of English middle class life' (W i 57).

The cramp he suffered was of a different sort. James Mill decided to teach his son himself, and he made few concessions to childish tastes. There were few children's books or toys, and no parlour games. Mrs Mill was an amiable but ineffectual woman who was quite unable to stand up to her husband's severity or make up for it in love and affection for her son. When he looked back on his boyhood many years afterwards, John could say nothing positive about her contribution and decided not to mention it at all. What he did recall was an unvarying regime of difficult books and daunting problems handed on to him by his father. He seems to have begun Greek at the age of three, Latin at eight. Before he was ten he had read through six of Plato's dialogues. He then began logic, in which his father had a special interest. There were breaks for lighter, but hardly for frivolous reading. John Mill read a great deal of history, he enjoyed *Robinson Crusoe*, and he was encouraged to read and even write poetry. But there was no unforced innocent saturation in imaginative literature for the sake of mere enjoyment; everything was subordinated to James Mill's didactic plan.

The manner of teaching was as demanding as the matter. Father and son worked at their respective tasks in the same room, and John was left to struggle with problems by himself, interrupting his father for help only when he dared. At the end of the day, they would take a walk, during which James Mill expected his son to give an account of what he had read and how much he had understood. Soon he had to put his knowledge to practical use. As his younger brothers and sisters grew up, John was required to supervise their lessons, and if they failed, to share their punishment. At a very early age he was being treated by his father as a sort of secretary. At thirteen he was introduced to political economy, with the *Principles* of David Ricardo. This James Mill expounded on walks, and John was expected to write up the discussion for his father's correction. The result was an introductory textbook, the *Elements of Political Economy*, published in 1820. By his late teens, John was participating in all his father's literary work. By 1823, when he took the post at the India House, he must have seemed a mere replica of James Mill.

An education of this sort would hardly have been possible if John Mill had not been quite unusually gifted. Probably the boy's quickness and capacity for mastering tough problems by himself encouraged his father to load him with more. And for all its severity this method did bring real benefits. It wasted no time on trivia. At twenty, John Mill was a generation ahead of his contemporaries. He was not daunted by large and intractable subjects, but trusted his own capacity to worry out their meaning patiently and systematically. He early assumed that the best way to master a subject was to write his own 'treatise' on it. His logical training prevented him from becoming a pedant, a mere repository of recondite information. 'The first intellectual operation in which I arrived at any proficiency, was dissecting a bad argument, and finding in what part the fallacy lay . . . an intellectual exercise in which I was most perseveringly drilled by my father' (W i 23). The daily *compte rendu* was a training in tenacity of memory and lucidity of exposition. He wrote clearer prose than his father from a very early age, and one of the most attractive things in his writings is the lucid presentation of difficult and abstract ideas. To the end of his life he wrote of the Socratic dialogue, not merely as a training in dialectical skill, but as the foundation of all scientific knowledge. His father's reliance on it, he insisted, had prevented his education from being one of mere 'cram'. His father had striven 'to make the understanding not only go along with every step of the teaching, but if possible, precede it' (W i 35). So John Mill's convictions were not mere dogmas, but carefully founded, defensible positions. He was, as one of his contemporaries noted, 'armed at all points'.

Of course this training brought its problems. Many people who met the younger Mill in his teens thought him a prig. Here was a boy who had no doubt that he was going to be a reformer of the world. Certain that he could expose the reasoning behind traditional beliefs and institutions he had gathered converts to his views, first through little discussion groups and societies, later in the wider forum of a debating society of young men of his own age. He was already, before the age of twenty, pouring out articles of considerable sophistication in newspapers and periodicals.

Some of his contemporaries called him 'a manufactured

man'. He himself once made the moving admission: 'I never was a boy, never played at cricket: it is better to let nature have her own way.' Many of Mill's readers have wondered if Nature did not have her own way, since Mill experienced a reaction against this too intellectual regimen, which led him to revise his views. But Mill's mature judgement in the *Autobiography* was that his case showed that difficult subjects can be thoroughly taught at a time of life when most children are taught nothing at all. The implication of this is that what he was taught so early, he retained. We cannot decide how far Mill departed from his training until we have sketched at least its main elements. If this seems to take up too large a part of a short book, we have the support of Mill's own example. By far the largest part of the *Autobiography* deals with the influences upon him before he was twenty-four, nearly half of it with those he experienced before he was twenty.

Describing the creed which he and his friends adopted, John Mill was careful to say that it 'was not characterized by Benthamism in any sense which has relation to Bentham as a chief or guide, but rather by a combination of Bentham's point of view with that of modern political economy, and with the Hartleian metaphysics' (W i 107). Let us consider these in turn, and examine the ethical and legal thought of Bentham, the political economy of Ricardo, and the psychological theory (then called metaphysics) and educational policy of his father James Mill.

Utilitarian ethics

John Mill first read Bentham in 1821, on his return from a year's stay in France. His father gave him the *Traité de Legislation*, the translation into French, by the Genevan Étienne Dumont, of Bentham's introductory view of a legal system. Reading this was a turning-point. 'I felt taken up to an eminence from which I could survey a vast mental domain, and see stretching out into the distance intellectual results beyond all computation' (W i 69). He learned for the first time of the 'principle of utility', which 'gave unity to my conceptions of things'.

The principle of utility (from which the popular name of the whole outlook rather confusingly derives) embraced both an ethical and a psychological theory. Bentham thought that the only things men desire for their own sakes are pleasure and the avoidance of pain. Men are egoists. The happiness they aim at *is* a preponderance of pleasure over pain. The same principle also provides them with a standard of conduct. An act is good if it produces or tends to produce more pleasure than pain. He who can calculate this most accurately is the most virtuous man: moral action is in fact the calculation, in units of pleasure and pain, of the consequences of an act. But of course men differ according to their circumstances in their conceptions of pleasure, and even the most far-seeing cannot predict all the consequences of a given act. What is needed, therefore, is a legislator who, taking self-interest as the universal motive, so orders men's relations in society that in benefiting himself each benefits the community of which he is a member. The legislator can assume that men in their private lives will regulate their conduct according to the principle of utility; his task is to extend this principle to society at large and show that it can produce 'the greatest happiness of the greatest number'. 'Private ethics', says Bentham, 'teaches how each man may dispose himself to pursue the course most conducive to his own happiness . . . the art of legislation teaches how a multitude of men, composing a community, may be disposed to pursue that course which upon the whole is most conducive to the happiness of the whole community, by means of motives to be applied by the legislator.'

Bentham devoted his whole life to this 'art of legislation'. The enterprise began in a coolly scientific spirit, but gathered more fanciful elements as it went on. Originally he had hoped, like Hobbes before him, to show that individual self-interest was perfectly consistent with law and order, indeed their only safe foundation. His basic assumption was a simple empiricism: 'The only objects which have any real existence are those which are corporeal.' To understand reality we had to reduce things to their smallest divisible components. Of course, for convenience, men grouped many things together under the same name, but these names were strictly speaking names for 'fictions'. There could be useful fictions, which conveniently described many things of the same sort, such as property, society, or nation. There were other misleading fictions which were not names for things but were commonly used as if they were. Such were duty, right, obligation, honour, community—dangerous words if used as if they stood for things with autonomous life. A community was nothing more than the sum of the individuals composing it. Individuals as a rule of their nature sought their own good, and so a community could have no interest at odds with the interests of its component members. Bentham thought that most social problems could be resolved, or at least a start made in their resolution, if such fictions could be shown for what they were. If by analysis general terms could be 'decomposed' into their elements, a rational vocabulary of political obligation could at last be devised, and a stable 'fabric of felicity' built upon it. Men had hitherto quarrelled over invulnerable nothings: teach them to give their attention to proven reality, and they could not fail to find a progressively larger measure of agreement.

At first this reductionism, this habit of decomposing things into their smallest elements, was directed at the fallacies, as Bentham conceived them, of contemporary liberalism. It was absurd, Bentham thought, to suppose states originated in some contractual agreement: that idea only generated confusion. A state was only a convenient device, best defined as a number of persons in the habit of obeying a governor. Law was the will or command of this governor. Obedience was acting in pursuance of that will. Law created both duties and rights. A duty was an expectation of punishment for not doing something; rights were powers for enforcing duties. These definitions Bentham used against what he considered the most fruitful source of dangerous fictions, the theory of natural rights proclaimed by the American and French revolutionaries, which he called, in a famous phrase, 'nonsense on stilts'. A state founded on the principle of utility would not need such fictions, because in such a state there could be no conflict between a man's duties and his interests. All law was in one way or another an infringement of liberty, and the best way of preserving such liberty as was compatible with order was to define the law, analysing its elements and thereby delimiting its functions. 'We must first know what are the dictates of legislation', says Bentham, 'before we can know what are the dictates of private ethics.' Personal liberty would be that area of conduct which the laws could not reach. This reversed the procedure of the theorists of natural rights. The security of the subject was best obtained, not by vague declarations of natural rights but by an exact, scientific reduction of law to its essentials.

It was here that Bentham sought to apply his analytical method to the language of the law. To obtain a rational legal system, he thought, we must first describe its subject-matter as a science does, by accurate, simple, yet exhaustive classification. The constituent elements of a legal system were the physical acts of individuals. These could be sorted into classes of act, so that one law would apply to one class. Legal penalties would be determined according to a utilitarian calculus, of the pain caused by the act in question. They would be preventive, threatening just so much pain as would deter the would-be malefactor from committing a crime, not retributive, for revenge was pain that could not be rationally calculated. It was the inconsistency and capriciousness of English law which Bentham most disliked, and he thought its technicalities were only a screen for exploitation and chicane. By giving different names to essentially similar acts (murder and manslaughter, for example) it introduced a confusing subjectivity into the assessment of punishment. Bentham's plan sought to eliminate these abuses. Its classification would be as clear and objective as the classification of the elements in chemistry. Its penalties would follow the great rule of utility. The law might thus be condensed into a single book, of which a man might say, 'Within this cover is the sole basis of my rights, the sole standard of my duties.' Armed with such an aid, the citizen would not need to buy a lawyer's specialist knowledge, for no knowledge would be needed that would not be available to all. Judges' discretion would be much reduced, and the common law, which Bentham regarded as a vast system of abuse, based on the fallacy that judges distilled a wisdom peculiar to themselves, would be replaced by a clear legal code.

That was the plan. Its application proved more difficult. Having thrust contemptuously aside the theorists of natural rights, Bentham failed to win over the lawyers with his scheme to recast the entire language of the law. The negative side of this, the purely destructive critique of current legal jargon, was very powerful. The positive side, the creation of a new and more accurate terminology, was largely a failure. Bentham had oddly anticipated this himself. 'Change the import of the old names', he had

9

written, 'and you are in perpetual danger of being misunderstood: introduce an entire new set of names, and you are sure not to be understood at all.' This is what happened, especially with his later writings. There, one suspects, readers have usually made a straight utilitarian choice, and judged the pains of mastering the new terminology to be greater than the pains of abiding by the old. Nor was this just a matter of literary taste, though that had much to do with it. A more fundamental objection to the new names was that they did not correspond to new things. As a science discovers new phenomena, it must invent new names to describe them. But Bentham's terminology did not work like this; it invented the names first. For a professed empiricist, he had a surprising disdain for the actual practice of the law, and for the social system in which it operated. The multiple categories into which he divided his subject were his own invention; they followed from his basic utilitarian purpose, to show how a self-interested man would work in a legal system which took self-interest to be universal. The professed aim was the reform of the law, but no one could credit the conclusions who did not accept the assumptions. So the logical culmination of the system was the construction of an elaborate but wholly imaginary model of a state, the *Constitutional Code*.

The *Code* was never completed, and it was read, if at all, only by members of Bentham's immediate circle. He seems to have realized that his demands were too radical for his countrymen, and as his plans ramified he developed his own forbidding jargon, quite as barbarous as the legal cant it was to replace, only less familiar. Originally meant as a more accurate and emotion-free terminology, its elaboration became a self-indulgent game and private refuge. It made his later writings so impenetrable that he came to rely on 'translators' to present his ideas to the public. This was not wholly his fault. It took a series of disappointments (routine reverses to a politician, but crippling to a man of Bentham's sensibilities) to turn this reputedly tough-minded social reformer into a fantasizing recluse. At first he had seen himself as an inventor, every bit as practical as an Arkwright or a Watt. He had planned a utilitarian system in miniature, a reformatory prison called the Panopticon, in which the prisoners were housed in insulated cells each open to the scrutiny of the gaoler. In this way, the operation of self-interest combined inexorably with the principle of publicity to reform the criminal, or at least convert him into a profit-making operative. Bentham had even dreamed of extending the principle and becoming the master of all the paupers and criminals in Britain, in a vast system of supervision and control. The Panopticon had been offered to the politicians, who toyed with it for a time and then turned it down. This was a turning-point for him. He concluded that society was so arranged that the men in power had no motive to recognize, much less pursue, the common good. The ruling groups—the aristocracy, the Church, and the lawyers—were leagued together in a common conspiracy against improvement, a network of 'sinister interests'. This explained why his arguments were ineffectual. He now took up the extreme radical programme of universal suffrage, annual parliaments and vote by ballot, and attacked the Church of England for its obscurantist attitudes. His friends feared, reasonably enough, that he would harm his reputation if he became associated with the radical movement at a time of popular violence.

They need not have worried. Bentham's later style was a form of censorship in itself. But in any case, he was never a simple radical republican. 'He merely passed', as the French historian Halévy pointed out, 'from a monarchic authoritarianism to a democratic authoritarianism,

11

without pausing at the intermediary position, which is the position of Anglo-Saxon liberalism.' He was always more fascinated by the machinery for controlling men than by the men themselves. For the prisoners in the Panopticon, and the paupers in the national scheme for poor-relief, he had planned a horrifying routine of unremitting supervision and direction. Accused of dehumanizing them and turning them into machines, he replied, 'Call them machines; so they were but happy ones, I should not care.' Absorbed in the elaboration of machinery which would convert men's self-love into general benefit, he gave little attention to the psychological needs of the individual. The conversion to republicanism was not therefore as great a change as might be supposed. The same publicity which he had proposed for the reformation of his prisoners pervaded every area of the democratic state of his imagination. 'Official aptitude' (that is, the probity and efficiency of the rulers) depended on their responsibility to those they ruled. The operation of this principle could be made still more certain if every official was required to work in the perpetual glare of public attention. So officials became the new prisoners, the public itself was vested with the task of gaoler, and a complex web of bureaucratic rules replaced the cell walls to prevent official collusion against the general good. It was the Panopticon turned inside out.

It was just this faith in rational planning, which to us makes Bentham the prophet of the modern bureaucratic state, which made him seem to his radical contemporaries so irrelevant or incomprehensible. Popular radicals misunderstood him, moderate reformers despaired of him, lawyers made fun of him. He became an eccentric recluse. 'In my country, of course, less said of me than in any other.' The 'of course' has a hint of complacency. Quite logically, he looked for the realization of his plans to revolutionary regimes abroad. A virgin territory, whose simple-minded inhabitants, without memories, would submit to the new set of institutions imposed by a revolutionary coup d'état, would be ideal. He considered Portugal, Spain, Greece, the New World.

But while his ambitions to be the legislator of these new republics brought him strange new followers and some public ridicule, it was his earlier disciples who ensured his enduring fame. Dumont's French versions probably gained Bentham a wider readership abroad than he ever enjoyed in Britain. James and John Mill applied his doctrines to the government of India, and it was through the latter's sympathetic criticism that most Victorians became acquainted with Bentham's ethical and legal doctrines.

Ricardian economics

Utilitarianism claims to judge the morality of an action by its consequences in pleasure and pain. But a knowledge of *all* the consequences of an act is hardly possible for the agent to achieve. However deliberately and scrupulously he commits an action, he may still be totally unprepared for its major consequences, which may even be the reverse of what he intends. We may be tolerably certain what effects an act will have in our own circle of intimates; but outside that, in our wider social relations and our behaviour as citizens, we need the help of more technical knowledge. In other words, a consequentialist theory of ethics like utilitarianism, if it is to be more than a rough rule of thumb, needs to be supplemented by the findings of social science. In Mill's youth the social science which seemed to have attained the greatest prestige and scientific precision was economics—or political economy as it was then called. And in the Mill circle, while Adam Smith was revered as the founder of the science, Ricardo was thought to have brought it near perfection. In so far as John Mill's education was directed

13

at making him a reformer of society, it was Ricardo's method that provided the model of social enquiry, and Ricardo's *Principles* the foundation of his economic theory.

It was a very different method from Bentham's. Ricardo was a self-taught stockbroker, not much given to theorizing about what he was doing, but James Mill, who did much to persuade him to complete the *Principles*, and whose advice he took about form and method, certainly had in mind Newtonian mechanics. Ricardo sought to describe the economic system of his day in a highly schematic and simplified form (what modern economists would call a model) in which a few premises were assumed, and from these certain long-term trends projected. To make the demonstration clearer, distracting details which might qualify the original hypothesis, and any statistical confirmation of its predictions, were ruthlessly pared away. 'My object', said Ricardo, 'was to elucidate principles, and to do this I imagined strong cases that I might show the operation of those principles.' The language was plain and spare; there was the greatest economy of illustration and example; the argument was highly condensed. The *Principles* is a forbiddingly abstract book. Its conclusions nevertheless served a clear political purpose.

There are three classes in Ricardo's system: the labourers, the landlords, and the capitalists, each with its characteristic form of gain, wages for labour, rent for land, and profit for capital advanced. Of the three, the labourers are in the least favourable position. For they, as the most numerous class, are most affected by the law, which Ricardo derived from the work of Malthus, that population increases much faster than subsistence. They live on the edge of destitution, and as soon as they experience an improvement in wages, they improvidently beget more children and so are soon reduced to want again. These fluctuations in their condition lead Ricardo to the chilling observation that the natural price of their labour is that which will enable them 'to subsist, and to perpetuate their race, without either increase or diminution'. But the capitalist is not much more favourably placed. He has capital to start with, but as the value of a commodity is determined by the amount of labour which has gone into producing it, this capital is in a sense not his own. It represents the rewards of past labour, or 'hoarded labour' as James Mill was to call it, and it must be advanced to the labourer in the form of wages, tools, machinery and raw materials, the profit being what is left. This profit moreover is precarious, being threatened first by competition from other capitalists eager to imitate any example of successful investment, and next by the constant demands of the labourer for higher wages. These demands it is not in the power of the capitalist to limit or control. For they are determined by the price of food, or more precisely by the price of bread. The only gainer in all this is the landowner. For he draws his rent from his land, and while his land will vary in its fertility, the market price of the grain it yields will be determined by the cost of producing grain on the poorest soils in cultivation. Wages being the same on fertile or infertile soil, the greater profit will accrue to the owner of the fertile soil, because there the yield costs less labour to obtain. While therefore the pressure of population leads to the cultivation of poorer and poorer lands, it is the capitalist who has to pay higher wages and receive lower profits. The landowner merely enjoys higher and higher rents. He is the only gainer from a world moving rapidly to economic stagnation, as wages rise, costs increase, and the incentive to investment flags.

Set out in crude outline in this way, the political purpose of the system is clear. Its main thrust was directed at the Corn Laws, which by imposing duties on foreign corn, kept up the home price and made it worthwhile for farmers to grow wheat on inferior upland soils. This might suit the country's needs while the war lasted, but with the coming of peace it seemed merely a cynical way of keeping up the high price of food in the teeth of industrial depression and popular distress. Ricardo's argument blamed the landed interest (dominant in parliament, as the 1815 Corn Law showed) both for the high price of the poor man's food and for the industrialist's sagging profits. Repeal the Corn Laws, allow imports of cheap foreign corn, and the price of bread would fall and profits would recover. 'I contend for free trade in corn', Ricardo wrote, 'on the ground that while trade is free, and corn cheap, profits will not not fall however great the accumulation of capital. If you confine yourself to the resources of your own soil, I say, rent will in time absorb the greatest part of that produce which remains after paying wages, and consequently profits will be low.' The landlords who received the rent, in other words, were inhibiting the investment of capital, and hastening the advent of the stationary state in which industry would stagnate. It was an argument both against the landed interest and the unreformed state of the parliamentary representation which gave landowners so much political power.

The mechanical rigidity of Ricardo's logic, and the political conclusion to which the argument pointed, seem all the more obvious to us now, because we know none of his predictions came about. The expansion of British industry was spectacular despite the Corn Laws. Population did not increase so fast that large numbers starved, even before the Laws were repealed. Living standards rose, and the birth-rate fell. But of course these developments lay in the future. To Ricardo's contemporaries what was convincing about his analysis was precisely its aloofness from politics. It seemed to penetrate the confusing welter of facts on the surface, to bypass the clamour of conflicting claims which various interested parties made from a partial appreciation of the facts, and to show, very clearly and objectively, the laws according to which the whole machine worked. Those laws had a political aspect, but that was not what made them authoritative so much as their simplicity, their logical consistency, and the indifference to party considerations of those who had found them out.

The political economists were hostile to state intervention. The economy should be allowed to work as its laws showed it would work best. Such political action as was needed should be limited to the removal of impediments to its working, not the creation of more. But that did not mean that the individual was to stand passively by and watch a process which might reduce him to destitution. When you know how a machine works, you can use it more effectively. If people could be shown the laws of political economy, they could learn how to use them to improve their lot. The laws were both explanations of complex phenomena and guides to action, principles as well as precepts. A good example is the 'principle of population', which Ricardo took from Malthus. Malthus claimed that while population increased in a geometrical ratio (1, 2, 4, 8, 16, 32 . . .), food did so only in an arithmetical one (1, 2, 3, 4, 5 . . .). There was no statistical evidence for this claim, which was in fact made before the first British population census. Though successive censuses provided the evidence of a spectacular rise in Britain's population, Malthus did not remove his chapter on the ratios from successive editions of his book. Not that Malthus thought that men were in the grip of a process over which they had no control. Rather he thought that if they knew about the principle they would see the point of controlling their appetites and having fewer children, or at least no more than they could support. This stress upon the individual's capacity to know the laws governing his own prosperity, pervades the whole Ricardian system. It is the core of what we call economic liberalism. The theory was at once individualistic, in leaving the individual master of his own destiny, and scientific, in claiming to find out by dispassionate, impartial enquiry, laws that lay in the nature of things.

In a famous passage, J. M. Keynes claimed that Ricardo's doctrine 'conquered England as completely as the Holy Inquisition conquered Spain'. He went on to describe the ingredients of this success.

> That it reached conclusions quite different from what the ordinary uninstructed person would expect, added, I suppose, to its intellectual prestige. That its teaching translated into practice, was austere and often unpalatable, lent it virtue. That it was adapted to carry a vast logical superstructure, gave it beauty. That it could explain much social injustice and cruelty as an inevitable incident in the scheme of progress, and the attempt to change such things as likely on the whole to do more harm than good, commended it to authority. That it afforded a measure of justification to the free activities of the individual capitalist, attracted to it the support of the dominant social force behind authority.

Historians of economic thought would now disagree with the last two sentences. Actually Ricardo's doctrines were being contested within a few years of his death. Even James Mill admitted that he and McCulloch were the only two men who could be truly called Ricardo's pupils, and later McCulloch came to differ sharply from his master. But the other ingredients Keynes noticed, the austerity, the unpalatable conclusions and the logical coherence of the system, certainly do explain its appeal to young men like John Mill.

Now this appeal had two most important consequences for utilitarianism; one political, the other theoretical. The political consequence was that for John Mill's generation, it neutralized the authoritarian element in Bentham's thinking. Utilitarianism is not necessarily a libertarian doctrine. If the goodness or badness of an action depends on its consequences, moral rectitude lies with the man who most accurately assesses those consequences. As governments are often better informed about the likely effects of certain activities, they must, at least in some areas, be better judges of what is right than the individual (who is usually misled by the will o' the wisp of conscience or the moral sense). Governments also have much more power than the individual to put their knowledge to effective use, so that even if they do not pursue the greatest happiness of the greatest number, they enlist the support of those who think they ought to.

Though Bentham paid lip service to the economic liberalism of Smith and Ricardo, his own economic writings show that he wanted the State to intervene in economic life in a manner contrary to their teaching. He wanted the Bank of England nationalized; he wanted governments to control education and research; he even wanted them to fix prices and guarantee a minimum wage, because 'insurance against scarcity cannot be left with safety to individual exertion'. The fact that these views remained unpublished and the divergence unnoticed has given a false impression of unanimity. Bentham's own fatuous remark that he was, through James Mill, the spiritual father of Ricardo, is typically misleading. In fact, he was at best a critical ally, and the main tendency of his thought lies in a different direction. His whole concern was with the mechanism of a legal and bureaucratic system which would so arrange its penalties or 'sanctions', that the individual would always be induced to pursue the public

19

good. He would act in his own interest spontaneously within a limited sphere, under legal sanctions outside that. The political economists were not concerned with devising elaborate legal disciplines. They thought that the competing selfishness of individuals created its own discipline, in the operation of a free market, and that the study of this market revealed the prevalence of laws which worked, whether men knew it or not, for the ultimate benefit of society. Both agreed that governments could do little in the economic sphere. But for Bentham this was because they could do more in the spheres of law and order, education and administration, whereas economic activities could regulate themselves. For the economists the economic activities formed the centre of the picture and the institutions of government were secondary; not because the latter were not indispensable, but because their economic pretensions had usually been harmful and there was no point in rendering them more efficient. Bentham wanted to remodel government with exactly that aim of greater efficiency, and the existing political instruments were mere obstacles to his plans of reconstruction. So he supported radical democrats at home and revolutionary dictators abroad. The Mills reconciled the contradiction rather better, because it fitted their double roles as imperial administrators and radical publicists. In his writings on India James Mill was a utilitarian interventionist, loading Benthamic plans on to the baggage-train of military conquest; but in British politics he favoured individualism and the free play of market forces. He justified this with a theory of history, according to which societies were destined to pass through successive phases of development, the more advanced being justified in showing the less advanced what was good for them, if necessary by force. We shall see the same tension between interventionism and *laissez-faire* in John Mill's thought, though there the reconciliation is much more subtle.

The theoretical consequence of the prestige of Ricardian economics was that it encouraged a deductive a priori approach to social and political problems. In principle, at least, one would expect a utilitarian social science to be experimental and inductive. The utility of existing institutions would be measured according to the pain and pleasure they promote; a proposed change would be held to advance the greatest happiness of the greatest number because it would bring about what most people actually want. To a large extent Bentham's mechanical assumptions about human nature and his growing aversion to reality prevented him from founding such a science. But the prestige of Ricardianism inhibited it still more. It presented exactly what those who hankered after a Newtonian science of society thought they wanted most: a reduction of human activity to a bare, skeletal set of laws, deduced logically from certain supposedly dominant traits of human nature, and owing their persuasiveness to the theoretical coherence of the system rather than its capacity to accommodate the variety of social life. The search for such laws, which were to stand in the same relation to society and the task of the politician as the laws of mechanics stood to the materials and projects of the engineer, became a distinguishing feature of the utilitarian outlook.

A famous example of the application of the Ricardian method to a practical problem, that of parliamentary reform, is James Mill's *Essay on Government*. Mill's argument actually starts with a rejection of historical evidence. As history provides no certain principles in such an enquiry, he says, we must go deeper, and look at human nature. Here we find that man is everywhere self-seeking and rapacious. The point of government, indeed, is that it keeps this rapacity in check. As there is no limit to men's appetite for 'the objects of desire' all governments in which power is vested in one man or in a few, will tend to oppress their subjects. The only way to secure good government is to identify the rulers with the whole community. Modern States cannot assemble all their citizens like ancient Athens, but they have something more practicable in 'the grand discovery of modern times, the system of representation'. But will not representatives, once vested with power, abuse it and oppress the community they are supposed to represent? James Mill agrees that they will, unless they are made answerable to the community by the devices of a wide suffrage and regular elections. These conditions echo the radical demand for universal suffrage and shorter parliaments, and there has been much argument about how far Mill wanted the vote extended, whether he wanted universal suffrage or something more restricted. The important point however is that he did not feel obliged to spell out what precise measures he wanted, any more than Ricardo had done. He was enunciating the basic principles of good government, and leaving it to others to draw the correct conclusions. He thought he had set out his argument so clearly that no one could fail to draw from it conclusions favourable to reform. But to have given his proposals in the form of legislative measures would not only have put him in the awkward position of agreeing with this or that brand of radical politician, but would have derogated from the self-appointed role of the austere philosopher who despised 'practical politicians'.

Associationist psychology

Bentham's and Ricardo's works do not seem, to put it mildly, written to secure a wide popular appeal, however democratic they were in principle. Their views needed another ingredient before they could be made part of a popular movement for reform. This was the psychological theory of associationism, which derived from Locke and David Hartley, was broadened in the following century by Rousseau and narrowed by Helvetius, and which finds its most uncompromising expression in the work of James Mill. In his hands it had the look of a doctrine deliberately chosen to fill a political need. He had been an enthusiastic supporter of a whole series of schemes for popular education, from primary schools based on the monitorial system to the tract-distributing Society for the Diffusion of Useful Knowledge, and finally the new London University. In all these activities, Mill had felt the need for a philosophical argument which would discredit those who held that popular education involved propagating 'dangerous' ideas subversive of established institutions, and which would at the same time give encouragement to his fellow reformers. He found this in associationism. Originally intended by Locke to combat the theological dogma (by no means dead in the early nineteenth century) that our ideas of good and bad are implanted in our minds by the Creator, it could be used more generally to support the reformers' contention that the differences between men in society are due to environmental factors and not to innate abilities. Already in 1817 Mill had projected a book in which he would 'make the human mind as plain as the road from Charing Cross to St. Paul's'. In 1820 he sketched its outline in the *Essay on Education*, in which he called for further philosophical work, but declared provisionally: 'this much, at any rate, is ascertained, that all the difference which exists, or can be made to exist, between one *class* of men and another, is wholly owing to education'. In 1822 he began the book which was to become the *Analysis of the Phenomena of the Human Mind*, and he found the investigation surprisingly straightforward. His arguments were vetted by his son, 'whose mind however is perfectly ripe to judge of them; and to him the expositions appear easy of comprehension, and perfectly satisfactory'. The book was finally published in 1829 and was discussed at the morning seminars by John Mill and his friends.

The theory in James Mill's hands is a mixture of psychology and philosophy. That is, it purports to describe how the mind works, but also to show that only certain forms of mental activity constitute real knowledge. It claims to be experimental, but by this is meant merely that the enquirer describes what passes in his mind through introspection, not that he uses experimental methods to show the nature of mental processes such as learning, memorizing, and so on. The mind is conceived, as it was by Locke, as a dark room, the senses being the windows which alone provide its knowledge of the external world. All we know therefore is dependent on the experience of our senses. Our knowledge of composite objects or complex ideas is really the stored knowledge of particular examples grouped together by association. The laws of association tell us how this grouping takes place, by contiguity, succession, and so on. Our abstract conceptions of good and bad, justice and injustice, are likewise resolvable into separate impressions, bound together by the experience of pleasure and pain. This is why moral convictions are susceptible to proof and disproof. The mind cannot resist the evidence of fact, any more than a mirror can resist reflecting an image of the object in front of it. A mere exposure to fact will precipitate a conviction. Moral convictions are more fallible, because the experience of pleasure and pain can be artificially associated with different objects. Put Oliver Twist among Fagin's pickpockets, and he will come in time to approve of theft. But the educated mind has two functions. It can recover past impressions and it can analyse them. Analysis of the sequences or 'trains' of association by which the mind received a particular idea, can separate certain sensations from the pain or pleasure with which they had originally been fused. In this way a rational man dissolves his prejudices, by showing them to be nothing more than factitious associations of certain feelings with certain facts.

No theory could put more stress on the importance of the environment in mental development. But 'the doctrine of the formation of character by circumstances', as John Mill called it, cuts two ways. On the one hand it points to complete control of the learning environment for the most effective teaching. It implies that a child's perceptions are unselective, and that in the development of the intelligence the vital role is played by the teacher, in arranging the environment so as to make the 'right' associations in the pupil's mind. This is not flattering to the original intelligence. One of John Mill's most vivid memories was of being told by his father that he would find he was ahead of other boys in his reading and information, but that this was not something to be conceited about, as it was due 'to the very unusual advantage which had fallen to my lot, of having a father who was able to teach me, and willing to give the necessary trouble and time' (W i 37). He adds that this opinion was 'exactly the truth and common sense of the matter', as if in the learning process the mentor was all-important and the pupil a mere receptacle of impressions.

One the other hand, the environmentalist doctrine presents the political reformer with an almost insuperable obstacle in society at large. James Mill admitted that the earliest impressions were the deepest, and that this confirmed the common opinion about the special susceptibility of 'the tender mind'. But if that is so, then adult minds must be set in a pattern of prejudices which will be harder to change. If education includes, as James Mill said it did, 'every thing which operates from the first germ of existence to the final extinction of life', then it must be a progressively more futile enterprise.

James Mill would not accept this conclusion, because it led to the kind of conservatism which he disliked in Burke. Burke claimed that our moral values are set long before we learn to consider them critically. Men did not derive their moral ideas direct from their own experience, and it was dangerous and impious to claim that they did. Prejudices represented the accumulated moral wisdom of the race and their prevalence in society, far from being a thing to be deplored, was a source of stability: 'Prejudice makes a man's virtue his habit, and not a series of unconnected acts.' For James Mill virtue was precisely a series of unconnected acts. A utilitarian must judge the goodness of an act by its consequences: 'To act, without regard to consequences, is the property of an irrational nature. But to act without calculation is to act without regard to consequences.' He did not deny that men made use of general moral rules in the ordinary business of life. But he did deny that these rules should be allowed to become a sort of second nature and override the duty to calculate consequences. When faced by a conflict between a general rule and a course leading to the greatest happiness, one should follow the latter.

James Mill thought that the fundamental task of the teacher was to associate pleasure with the general good. But as his son noted, he had scarcely any belief in pleasure, and tended to identify it with what a man deliberately approves. He therefore gave Bentham's utilitarianism a very puritanical twist. Bentham wanted to harness men's egoism to drive an intricate political machine: James Mill wanted to eradicate egoism altogether, by a careful education, which was aimed to produce an alert, critical, and altruistic frame of mind. The principle of utility in his hands sheds it hedonistic elements and becomes almost an ascetic ideal. It 'marshals the duties in their proper order', Mill declares, 'and will not permit mankind to be deluded, as so long they have been, sottishly to prefer the lower to the higher good, and to hug the greater evil, from fear of the less'.

Was there not a rather undemocratic élitism lurking in this attitude of high-minded distaste for the 'sottish' preferences of the bulk of mankind? Certain passages in James Mill's works may suggest this. He was, for instance, a great admirer of Plato, and in the work just quoted he praises *The Republic* as a masterly development of his own principle, that the only security for good government is the identity of interest between rulers and ruled. It is clear that he admires the sort of education that Plato planned for his guardian class. But he goes on to say that the only reason Plato was forced to advocate a special status and a condition of propertyless celibacy for this class, was that he lived before the discovery of representative government. The implication of this seems to be that if Plato's guardians could become rulers in Mill's society, they would be good ones, but that a wide franchise would ensure their integrity quite as effectively as devices like celibacy or community of property. In other words, provided you have rulers accountable to the public, there is no need to fence their virtue with such artificial devices as Plato envisaged.

This faith in representation rested on the belief that all men were equally capable of receiving and understanding the truth. What prevented them from acting on that understanding was the fact that men were grouped in classes or interests. The aristocracy, with its supports, the Church and the Law, represented the three great threats to enlightenment, being essentially accretions of what Bentham had called 'interest-begotten prejudice' which corrupted men's opinions. Their baneful influence was artificially prolonged by an unrepresentative political system. Their long sway accounted for the moral backwardness, the 'sottishness' of mankind.

James Mill sometimes wrote as if this system could only be overthrown by political means, but in general (and especially as he rose in official rank and acquired more knowledge of the world of politics) he trusted to the influence of education which, slowly but inexorably, would persuade the ruling classes that their own best interests lay in pursuing the general good. He always remained, in spite of his official duties, a teacher rather than a politician, keeping aloof from political agitations and preferring to give his energies to education and the Press. It was in fact his pedagogic attitude which made him so naive in his political pronouncements. He had the teacher's characteristic failing of favouring those who agreed with him, and his didacticism biased his whole view of the political process. Those who agreed with him were the children of light. They had taken pains with their understandings; they did not live on the labour of others; they held the corrupting aristocracy at arm's length; and with their own hoarded labour (also called capital) they advanced good causes in such a way as to evoke the trust of their inferiors. They were the 'middle rank' who Mill thought formed the opinions of 'a large proportion of the whole body of the people'. James Mill would have denied that this middle rank was a class held together by an 'interest-begotten prejudice' of a new sort. Theirs was the legitimate influence of science and moral worth, and it could only grow with the growth of virtue; whereas the influence of the aristocracy was illegitimate, being based in the last resort on ignorance and deception, and would give way, as society improved 'under the guidance of educated intelligence' (W i 109).

James Mill used to be considered a mere popularizer of Bentham's work, and John Mill's eventual divergence from the doctrines of his youth as essentially a disillusionment with 'Benthamism'. But this picture now needs revision.

James Mill may not have been a very original thinker, but he was a great systematizer and teacher. His debt to Bentham was no greater than his debt to Ricardo or even Locke and Hartley. But the important thing was that he tried to weld these influences into a coherent social and political philosophy, which was made more formidable by his powerful didacticism. This philosophy, it is sometimes forgotten, loomed so large in John Mill's education that it left very little room for any other sorts of influence. There cannot be much doubt that his boyhood views were identical with his father's. What is less often admitted is that when he came to diverge from his father on particular issues, the ideal remained very similar. He may have developed a more indulgent view of the aristocracy and a more subtle one of the Church. He certainly came to question his father's faith in democracy. But on the central ideal, of a society ruled by its wisest and most virtuous members, father and son were at one.

2 Mental crisis and aftermath

At first, in the period of 'youthful propagandism' before he was twenty, John Mill was all confidence in the creed in which he had been brought up. He wrote and spoke with the dogmatism of a precocious adolescent, and he enjoyed the feeling of belonging to a movement with other young men who admired the work of Bentham and his father. They formed a little party of zealots, and Mill summarizes their views in his *Autobiography*. Their basic principles were a belief in representative government and freedom of discussion. They did not advocate a democratic system from a belief in natural rights, but because it seemed to them the only sure way to have good government. Their chief enemy was aristocracy, which they regarded as more formidable than monarchy, because it was more pervasive, and was abetted by the two great systems of corruption, the Established Church and the Law. Only if the general interest was mobilized against these two systems could they be destroyed, and the first step was to expose their pretensions by challenging them to open debate. The young utilitarians had no doubt that their own mentors gave them the advantage in argument. The two ancient universities, after all, where the aristocracy and clergy were mostly educated, taught archaic curricula full of exploded superstitions and narrow classical learning, and so could never present a serious intellectual opposition. Already Cambridge had produced notable converts to utilitarianism. The walls of the citadel had been breached. Once deprived of the support of the Church and the Law, the landed aristocracy would be easier to convert to the truth that their best hope of survival lay in the pursuit of the general good.

Mill and his friends were not democrats in feeling. They respected property as an institution, and none of them was poor. Some, like George Grote the banker, were very wealthy. All were liberally educated and this, along with the recondite reading of the utilitarian canon, made it hard for them to reach down to the popular mind. They did not, like the Russian intelligentsia later in the century, sentimentalize the masses; their democratic faith consisted more of a dislike of aristocracy than a positive love of the common man. They hoped that the common man would be able at least to grasp the main conclusions of political economy and utilitarianism, and without presuming to interfere in the deliberations of his betters, be capable of distinguishing the honest from the dishonest among public men. They trusted in an enlarged electorate (covering at least the classes which could be reckoned to have the public good at heart) as a critical audience inducing probity in politicians, but hardly providing them itself. They wanted secret voting because that would at one stroke deprive 'the Few' of the means of intimidating 'the Many', and foster the independent judgement of the latter. Education for them did not mean only the spread of literacy, but also a heightening of political consciousness. Their empiricism led them to look on this as an irresistible process: as knowledge was diffused, people would become clearer about the choices before them, and the more these choices were made in the light of scientific fact, the more irreversible moral advance would be. They all agreed that this called for a programme of popularizing the new sciences of political economy, ethics, and jurisprudence. They were less good at putting this into effect. Their philosophic habit of mind, and their puritanical distaste for the more popular forms of literature (fiction was frivolous and poetry was misrepresentation) restricted their range as propagandists. They were strongest in abstract argument, and the journals in which they wrote were heavy going, dealing in matters which would nowadays be confined to academic periodicals. They saw themselves as playing a role like that of the Encyclopaedists in eighteenth-century France; but they had less variety and originality, and they came from a narrower stratum of society. Their fierce theoretical hatred of the aristocracy excluded them from the worlds of fashion and high politics, and seminars were no substitute for salons. But what they lacked in literary finesse they made up in zeal.

No one threw himself into the common cause with more energy than John Mill. He was their most gifted theorist and their standard of utilitarian orthodoxy. Then, quite suddenly, he lost all zest for the fray. One day he asked himself if it would make him happy to see realized all the ideals he had been brought up to consider right, and was horrified to find that his answer was 'No'. This plunged him into the deepest depression, for it seemed to show that his education had failed. He tried various remedies in vain. His favourite reading had lost its savour. So had music: he was even distressed by the thought of 'the exhaustibility of musical combinations' (W i 149). He could confide in no one, least of all his father. Walks did no good. He managed to carry on with his duties and even with his writing, but felt no enthusiasm for either. What oppressed him continually was the thought that he had lost all capacity to feel, that an analytical education had worn away his emotions. Finally, reading a book of French memoirs, and coming upon a particularly moving passage, he shed tears. This was a great relief, because it showed him that his feelings were not quite dead, and from that moment the depression began to lift.

The description of this 'mental crisis' is the most striking passage in the *Autobiography*. It has more depth and immediacy than the later encomium of his wife, which even Mill's admirers find rather excessive. It also contrasts so sharply with the dry complacency of Mill's account of the other intellectual influences upon him that many readers have concluded that the episode, so pivotal in the book, must represent a decisive break in his life, involving a strong emotional and intellectual revulsion against his education and traceable in all his later work. It seems likely that the depression was caused by overwork. The overwork involved not only writing learned reviews, debating and campaigning for birth-control, but editing from manuscripts the monumental five volumes of Bentham's *Rationale of Judicial Evidence*, a task which took him a year. Those who have groped about in the crepuscular world of Bentham's later writings, and know the sensation they give of systematic estrangement from the world of ordinary discourse, can readily imagine the impact of this dreary chore upon a youth buoyed up with the wish to better his society. It cannot, surely, have increased his relish for reforming causes.

But treating the 1826 crisis as the start of a 'revolt' against Mill's inheritance has its difficulties. For one thing, very little evidence has survived to amplify the account in the *Autobiography*. For a long time after 1826 he wrote little, and when he resumed writing, about 1830, he was not free to say exactly what he thought. He remained very much under his father's tutelage, submitting some of his views to James Mill's censorship, and carefully keeping other work anonymous. This means that, though in the ten years between the mental crisis and his father's death in 1836, Mill wrote a good deal about the work and opinions of his various mentors, it is very hard to be sure whether his comments are to be read as expressions of open rejection, covert criticism, or merely the reaffirmation of one part of his heritage against another. This last possibility, which is also the most likely, is usually ignored by those who assume that the ideas in which he was educated formed a logically coherent system, altering one part of which implied overhauling the whole. Through all his changes of mind, Mill remained remarkably faithful to his father's ideals, and in fact came increasingly to identify himself with them as he grew older. His criticisms of his heritage were sharpest in the 1830s; thereafter he became more and more convinced that the ideals he had been taught had been, at least in essentials, right. It is this that makes the *Autobiography* unreliable as an account of his feelings during and after the crisis. For all the signs are that it was written to vindicate the view which Mill sets out in Chapter 2, book VI of the *System of Logic*, that though we are in general shaped by circumstances, yet we can, if we wish, alter those circumstances to make ourselves what we want to be. Mill admitted some faults in his upbringing, but on the whole he came to believe that he had been taught to think for himself, and that the crisis of 1826, which he had once thought an indictment of his training, had led in the end to its vindication.

It is true that John Mill made something of a public renunciation of 'Benthamism'. He resigned from the Debating Society in 1829 after a bitter debate in which his beliefs were attacked, and after that he often denied that he was a Benthamite or Utilitarian. There may have been an element of real disillusionment here. It was undoubtedly a shock to discover that the doctrines he had thought self-evidently true and socially regenerative in fact aroused passionate opposition from young men like himself whom he respected and wanted to like; and he must often have wanted time for reflection and reconsideration of his heritage. In the same year, he had the extra shock of reading a powerful attack by Macaulay on his father's *Essay on*

Government, an attack which seems all the more conclusive for the relative feebleness of the published replies. But what prompted his resignation was not a wish to capitulate to his critics. It was the feeling that debating did not advance the truth, but was only a rhetorical battle in which the contestants had to caricature each others' views. As utilitarian champion he was called on to defend positions he did not always hold, with weapons he no longer liked to use, and so to make enemies of people he wanted to convert. The best and most honest thing to do was to shed the sectarian label, try to draw attention to the real views behind it, and advance these views by temperate discussion among friends, away from the unreal combat of the Debating Society. He did not give up his beliefs, but in the cooler atmosphere of the morning seminars he laid them on the table for discussion.

His name for this new course was 'practical eclecticism'. Later, borrowing a word from Goethe, he called it 'manysidedness'. Of course it involved making friends with men who, a few months before, he had considered opponents. Some of his fellow-utilitarians shook their heads and sniffed desertion, and outwardly at least they had a case. Mill became intimate with two notable disciples of Coleridge, John Sterling and F. D. Maurice, who were outspoken critics of associationism and utilitarian ethics. He became fascinated by Thomas Carlyle, whose writings made vehement fun of 'Benthamism', and who was mainly responsible for making the connection, which became a romantic cliché and has remained a socialist one, between the utilitarian outlook and the faith in machinery characteristic of the early factory system. He made friends with the young disciples of the French sociologist Saint-Simon, which was to lead to a long-lasting interest in the work of the most famous of the group, Auguste Comte. Finally, there was Harriet Taylor, the young married bluestocking with whom he fell in love and eventually married, to whom he attributed an influence over his opinions far exceeding that of all the others put together.

All these friendships may suggest Mill was straying from the straight and narrow path of utilitarianism. In fact, they show something rather more subtle. He had come to believe that one cannot be really confident of the truth of one's opinions unless one has given a fair hearing to those who hold the opposite. Neither Bentham in his insulated studies, nor James Mill in his confident dogmatism seems to have entertained such an idea. But John Mill was so impressed with it that he took it to mean that he must meet an opponent more than half-way. His correspondence with both Carlyle and Comte shows this. He is at first so open-minded, so self-deprecating, and so anxious to please that he is mistaken for a disciple. Seeing that he is in a false position he issues a qualified warning, but so diffidently that it is brushed aside. Presuming he has a captive audience the new friend avows still less guarded views. Horrified, Mill is driven to a more candid statement of their differences. The result is a mutual cooling of enthusiasm, the start of secret recrimination, which ripens into open hostility. It is not that Mill abandons his own views, but that with his acute impressionableness and naive appetite for controversy he plunges in, taking no account of the differences of personality and temperament which promise later divergence. His former friends and allies, not sharing his complex reasoning but judging by the company he keeps, conclude that he has deserted to the enemy.

But Mill was much too thoroughly versed in the doctrines he had been taught to throw them over; even had he wanted to, he had no other vocabulary in which to express himself. The most he sought to do was to make his inherited opinions seem less dogmatic. Eclecticism was a device to gain more converts. As Alan Ryan puts it, he wanted 'to expand, not to renounce his inheritance'. The picture we should have is not that of a young dogmatist being dislodged by powerful attacks from a rigidly held position. It is rather a case of his holding the same general ground, but realizing that some parts of it were vulnerable, and seeking to make the defences more flexible and stronger as occasion arose. By the end he had fashioned a deeper and more subtle version of the whole inheritance, and come to feel that, armed with it, he could meet at least those critics who acknowledged the same rules of controversy as he did. The overall purpose remained the same, to be a reformer of the world.

In what ways then did Mill 'expand his inheritance'? There were three main problems to confront. The first concerned the rival claims of intuition and associationism, and centred on the place of poetry in an education. The second followed from this, and involved a revision of utilitarian ethics. The third was concerned with the problem of authority in politics, why some men rule others, and how their rule can be reconciled with progress. This took longest of all, for the practical business of pressing for greater popular participation in politics was constantly hampered by the logically prior problem, whether politics could be made a science which the common people could understand.

Poetry and intuition

One of Mill's discoveries during the crisis of 1826 was that his analytical education had been very one-sided, developing the critical powers at the expense of the feelings (W i 141). The recovery of his capacity to feel which marked the ending of the crisis was a relief to him because it showed that analysis had not been totally destructive. Thereafter the problem was, how to keep faint feelings alive and even strengthen them. This was where Mill turned to poetry. He read Wordsworth for the first time in 1828 and thought that in this 'poet of unpoetic natures' he had found that 'culture of the feelings' he needed. This was in itself a departure from the critical attitude of the utilitarians towards poetry and poets. Bentham had said poetry was as good as 'pushpin'. James Mill in his *History* had tried to show that Hindu culture was backward and corrupt in spite of its beautiful Sanskrit poetry, by arguing that poetry was the characteristic expression of barbarous people who 'feel before they speculate', and which must necessarily give way to prose as scientific knowledge advances. He did not think that the imagination of the poet worked in any special way which distinguished it from that of the lawyer or the businessman. Imagination was any train of associations not set in motion by an external stimulus. Because poets habitually misread the evidence of the external world James Mill thought they made bad moral guides: 'Homer is the greatest of poets: where shall we place him among the moralists?' From their mentors the younger utilitarians drew that mixture of captious literalness and moral disapproval which marks the treatment of poets in the *Westminster Review*.

The followers of Coleridge however gave a much more important role to the poet than the utilitarians. In conscious revolt against the mechanistic philosophy which had 'untenanted creation of its God', they spoke of the poet as a moralist and seer, whose imagination gave men back their wonder and awe and appreciation of beauty, in spite of science. The poet perceived truths intuitively, and set them out in a form which all mankind could perceive directly and take to heart. A poetic fancy was one of the salient characteristics they approved of in their friends, a sign that a person could rise above the merely materialistic apprehension of life. For Maurice and Sterling poetry came to have more importance than theology. They found Mill amazingly prosaic, a 'manufactured man', and they looked hopefully for the growth of his imaginative powers.

Mill met the same outlook in Carlyle, who gave it strongly Germanic overtones and tremendous ironic force. Mill had been taught to believe that for an idea to be grasped it had only to be set out in clear, consecutive argument, and that analysis could dissolve all obscurities. Carlyle on the contrary believed, and with some success practised, the doctrine that elaborate philosophizing generated confusion and cant, and that for an opinion to be worth attending to it must be set down in a vivid and graphic way to match the immediacy of the original perception. His work was in manner and intention the antithesis of Mill's, and was replete with forceful criticisms and sardonic mockery of the latter's opinions.

As long as he felt he lacked a faculty which others had, Mill was very vulnerable to this sort of criticism. But meeting Harriet Taylor must have made him aware that his emotions no longer needed watering with the thin nutrient of Wordsworth, and he was encouraged to state his position in relation to the new influences. He could not repudiate his debt to poetry; he did not want to undervalue the writings of Carlyle and others, which he continued to feel were more vivid and inspired than anything he could manage. But he did want to assure himself that poetry must tell truth of some sort, and have some usefulness to mankind. Even if the poet reached the truth by a quicker route than other men, those others must have some warrant that it was the truth, even if it took them longer to grasp it. So he decided that what the poet did was describe his own emotions in language calculated to arouse similar emotions in others. A poet was a person with 'a peculiar kind of nervous susceptibility' which made his impressions particularly 'vivid and distinct' (W i 413). But he needed an interpreter and for this role Mill proposed himself. He told Carlyle that he conceived his own task to be that making the truths perceived by the higher natures available to the lower—through the unlikely medium of logic. Later he seems to have changed his mind and decided that the really great poets must not only deal in mellifluous language apt to convey emotion, but also be deep thinkers. In a review of Tennyson he admonished the poet to read more philosophy if he wanted to improve his poetry. Mill was not primarily a literary critic, and he did not reprint all these essays. They are of interest mainly in showing the relatively slight effect his romantic and poetic phase had upon his thought. It amounts to the rather meagre admission that poetry as the 'culture of the feelings' ought to have a larger place in a philosophic education, not because it was a source of knowledge, but because it could offer a counterweight to the dissolving effect of analysis. Mill never explicitly admitted that poets were born rather than made, or had any intuitive grasp of truth. Even their peculiar temperament he explained in associationist terms.

There was another, minor, effect of his interest in poetry. It explains his extraordinary reverence for Harriet's mind. If the poet was a person endowed with a peculiar kind of nervous sensibility, the converse was also true. Hence his conviction that she resembled Shelley, though he, 'so far as his powers were developed in his short life, was but a child compared with what she ultimately became' (W i 195). This was because, in her mastery of practical issues and her swift decisiveness in domestic matters, he discerned the qualities of a great statesman.

Utilitarian ethics

Another effect of the mental crisis was the realization that Bentham's egoistic psychology and the ethics drawn from it were quite inadequate. This may reflect a growing sense of the divergence between Bentham's views and James Mill's, and a perception that shedding Bentham's egoistic hedonism did less damage to the whole system of utilitarianism than any other concession. But it was upon that part of James Mill's work which is most Benthamic that the heaviest blow fell. In his attack on the *Essay on Government* Macaulay had pointed out that the claim that men were actuated by self-interest was an identical proposition: it merely amounted to saying that a man would rather do what he would rather do. Men had different conceptions of their interests, according to their different experiences and situations in life, so any attempt to take this as the foundation of a political science was building on sand. In his 'Remarks on Bentham's Philosophy', John Mill echoed Macaulay's criticism, but of course as a point against Bentham: 'There is nothing whatever which may not become an object of desire and dislike by association' (W x 13). By saying that all men were governed by their interests Bentham was only saying that 'all persons do what they feel themselves disposed to do'. The effect of this use of the word 'interest' only encourages the 'vulgar usage' which equated it with 'selfishness and miserable self-seeking'. A crude conception of motive led to an equally crude conception of moral good. Bentham's indifference to the way we acquire our moral standards accounted for the fact that he had no place in his system for conscience or duty. He ignored the fact that one factor in the calculus of consequences of an action might be the effect on the character of the agent himself. This was not a serious defect in his legal philosophy; for law is more concerned to deter crime than analyse the character of the criminal. But such a theory failed altogether in questions of national policy, let alone the grand design of carrying a community towards perfection (W x 9, 12–16). Five years later Mill elaborated the charge that Bentham's ethics applied only to *la petite morale*, the merely business side of human life. His idea of the world was 'that of a collection of persons pursuing each his separate interest or pleasure, and the prevention of whom from jostling one another more than can be helped, must be attempted by hopes and fears derived from three sources—the law, religion and public opinion'. Self-education, the training of the individual's affections and will, was 'a blank in Bentham's system' (W x 97–9). In other words, Mill rejected the Benthamic conception of a rational society as one operating on the principle of enlightened self-interest.

It was easier to blame Bentham for a crude and easily travestied version of utilitarianism than to show that the creed was compatible with high moral ideas and humane culture. Mill's new friends derived these from religious belief, and they thought the utilitarian philosophy was hostile to altruism in private ethics as well as the ideal of public service in politics. You could not be a utilitarian and a high-minded gentleman. Mill, too, valued an altruistic and cultivated ruling class, though he derived the ideal from classical Greece rather than Christianity: he wanted to keep the culture and shed the religion. He had fitted poetry into his programme without any concessions to 'mysticism' or intuitionism. Now he wanted the ethical standards which he admired in Greek philosophy to be shown to be amenable to proof. Bentham's felicific calculus would not do. His father's *History of British India* used the principle of utility as the measure of the progress of different peoples from barbarism to civilization, but while that might justify their joint efforts at the India House on the behalf of the backward subcontinent, it would not explain why highly cultivated young Englishmen like Sterling repudiated utility as a guide to action. What Mill sought was a version of utilitarianism which would combine ethical refinement and sophistication with an objective test of the morality of an act.

He was to find it eventually in the doctrine (essentially an elaboration of his father's version) of higher and lower pleasures which he first set out in *Utilitarianism*. There he held that the idealist who sought the good of mankind was still after pleasure, but of a higher order, and that an educated man faced with a choice between a refined pleasure like poetry and a coarse one like beer-drinking would always prefer the former. So it was, in a famous phrase, 'better to be Socrates dissatisfied than a fool satisfied' (W x 212). But that—Mill's major divergence from Bentham's utilitarianism—was a later development (the phrase first occurs in a diary entry for 1854). In the 1830s he was more concerned with another aspect of the Master's cultural legacy. This concerned the relation of utilitarianism to political economy. In his anxiety to show that utilitarians were not just concerned with 'the merely business side of human life', Mill had to contend with those who said, in effect, that the faith he and his friends expressed in political economy proved that they were. Again, this put him in a dilemma. He wanted to affirm his new-found sense of the value of a wide culture, but he did not want to question the value of political economy as a science. He therefore made a distinction between science and art. Science studies what is. Art studies how things are done. 'The language of science is, This is, or, This is not; This does, or does not happen. The language of art is, Do this; Avoid that. Science takes cognizance of a *phenomenon*, and endeavours to discover its *law*; art proposes to itself an *end*, and looks out for *means* to effect it' (W iv 312). So political economy, as a science, merely *describes* a particular area of human life and the laws which might prevail in it: it *prescribes* nothing, though its data might be essential to the prescriptions of morality.

Morality is not a science, but a branch, with prudence and aesthetics, of the Art of Life. In this, morality is concerned with imperatives, prudence with self-regarding precepts, and aesthetics with beauty or loveableness. Mill did not elaborate this classification. It functions in his work as a way of acknowledging areas of experience which utilitarians were usually accused of neglecting, while he gave his main efforts to those sciences on which the Art of Life depended. It also explains how in his final verdict on Bentham he was able to condemn him for shortcomings as a moralist yet praise him as the scientist who first classified the phenomena of the law, a sort of Linnaeus of the legal system.

Authority and progress

The new stress on self-culture also brought about a revision of Mill's attitude to traditional institutions. Instead of deducing from the 'known laws of human nature' the evils of aristocracy, Church, and Law, as he had done in his propagandist days, he developed a new feeling for society as a historic fabric, and he began to look more sympathetically at what he had once considered its 'interest-begotten prejudices'. Here the two great influences were the work of Coleridge and of Saint-Simon and his disciple Auguste Comte. One was romantic and conservative, the other was scientific and what would later be called positivist. Both helped Mill reformulate what he had first imbibed from Plato, a concern with fostering an élite leadership, not in the traditional shape of an aristocracy, but in the more modern one a trained and cultivated body of experts. The main question for Mill was how this body of experts could be both free to use their knowledge and responsible to the wider public whom they served.

The main idea Mill took from Coleridge was that of the 'clerisy'. In his tract *On the Constitution of Church and State* (1830) Coleridge set out his version of the doctrine of the three estates of the realm. The first consisted of the possessors of landed property and provided the element of law or 'permanence'. Merchants and manufacturers made up the second, and provided the element of 'progression'. The third was the clergy, who were the guardians of civilization, and made sure that there was something to preserve. For them was reserved what Coleridge called the 'Nationalty'—that portion of the national wealth not owned by the other two estates and explicitly reserved for the clergy by the nation, not to serve the narrow interests of the priesthood, or to ensure a doctrinal orthodoxy, but to cultivate and extend knowledge. Coleridge pointed out that in medieval Christendom the word clerk was used for all men of learning, and he argued that the modern Church would be more easily defended if it could recover something of its former comprehensiveness. Hence 'clerisy', a term which he hoped would convey the range of concern which 'clerk' or 'clergy' had lost.

What attracted Mill in this view of the English past was, first, that it gave a new and flatteringly large role to the thinker and man of letters. Once he had admitted that some people's opinions could count for more than others', Mill became alarmed at the danger of majority-rule. A majority might be that of the most ignorant mass, and this would be a threat to the ideal of self-cultivation and its political corollary, rule by the best-informed. Coleridge offered a way of counterbalancing the strength of the numerical majority. His three estates were more plausible historically than the utilitarian view of the constitution as an aristocratic fraud, and more in tune with Mill's new mood. Set out with great learning, and calculated to soothe the antagonism of commerce towards landed wealth, and of dissent towards the established Church, Coleridge's theory offered an ideal of social harmony without denying the need for reform. Society so balanced would still change, but the monitors of the change would be the clerisy.

The Coleridgeans were more interested in re-educating the possessing classes than in the superficial crash-programme which the 'useful knowledge' school urged to prepare the property-less for political responsibility. Such attempts to popularize science would, Coleridge said, only ensure its 'plebification'. More urgent was a dialogue *within* the clerisy. In his new mood Mill welcomed this as a bridge between his own views and those of Sterling and Maurice, and a more congenial task than the 'diffusion of superficial knowledge' which was the educational element in the radical programme. That, he now said, so far from being the march of intellect, was 'rather a march toward doing without intellect, and supplying our deficiency of giants by the united efforts of a constantly increasing multitude of dwarfs' (W i 330). Mill now sounded a note of distaste for popularization which contrasts sharply with his father's view that the reformer's prime duty was to popularize what was known. 'When almost every person who can spell, can and will write, what is to be done?' (W xxi 53). The real purpose of education was to make people think for themselves, not to indulge them with bald summaries and crude slogans; fostering genius for future discovery was more important than spreading what was known (W i 337–8).

Some of the Saint-Simonians affected the costume and ritual of a religious cult, but this was primarily as a means of harnessing a popular following. The core of their doctrine was scientific, and it was aimed, even more than Bentham's, at the reorganization of society on the principles of physical science. Saint-Simon's ideal society is the utopia of the frustrated inventor. He thought that as scientists, engineers, industrialists, and the various craftsmen whom they directed, created society's wealth and ensured its progress, they should govern it, and they would do the job better than the kings, aristocrats, and higher clergy, who had traditionally wielded power. For the only true knowledge was scientific; and the only real advances in men's understanding of their situation (as against the fitful intuitions and lucky guesswork of moralists and preachers) had been achieved by the physical sciences. So the only authority which had a right to command men's allegiance was that of the man of science. All other claims were archaic, the relics of previous ages' attempts to identify authority with knowledge, which had succeeded only in vesting it in various personifications of superstition. One could indeed, by marking off the successive stages by which mankind had emerged from superstition, demonstrate the underlying historical law. There were, said Comte, three stages through which all societies were bound to pass: the theological in which men attribute changes in the world around them to the actions of their gods; the metaphysical, when they explain them by reference to abstract forces; and the positive, when they come to understand them according to the laws of cause and effect—that is, by science. This was the scheme of development which Comte was to elaborate in the next fifteen years, and it seems to have made relatively little impact on Mill in the period immediately following the crisis of 1826. What made more impact on him was the Saint-Simonian division of history into organic and critical periods. Organic periods were those in which a particular creed dominated men's minds, and the authority of its teachers was generally accepted. Critical periods were those ages of transition when a creed was being outgrown, and men, no longer able to believe the old doctrines, cast about to find new ones. The Saint-Simonians said that the present age was a critical one, and they were confident that the organic age to follow would be one in which their own doctrines would hold sway.

Mill was wary of the Saint-Simonians' claims to form a new priesthood. He was not going to be identified with another 'sect'. But he liked the distinction between critical and organic periods, because, by identifying the present age as one of transition, it seemed to justify his interest in other creeds than his own, and fitted in with his preference for discussing principles rather than programmes. Some writers have seen this as a conversion to reactionary and conservative views, but it amounts to little more than a historical explanation of his current disillusionment with radical polemic. He still believed that his own views, suitably qualified but in essentials unchanged, would prevail; but he wanted to be open-minded rather than polemical about them, and he thought of the social changes he wanted as coming about, not by direct political action, but as a result of a long period of discussion. 'In the present age of transition', he told Sterling, 'everything must be subordinate to *freedom of enquiry*: if your opinions, or mine, are right, they will in time be unanimously adopted by the instructed classes, and *then* it will be time to found the national creed upon the assumption of their truth' (W xii 77). On his side Mill undertook to re-educate his fellow utilitarians, especially to a true appreciation of what was right in the creed of their opponents. The most enduring of his writings reflecting this desire are the essays on *Bentham* and *Coleridge*, written in 1838 and 1840. In each Mill tries to put the opposite view as clearly as his own. Bentham is severely criticized, often from a point of view congenial to the romantic critics of the Coleridgean persuasion, for his want of imagination and so on. Coleridge is highly praised as an equally profound thinker on the other side, and the sort of Tory whom Liberals need to know better if they are to attain a proper appreciation of their own shortcomings. These two essays are the supreme expression of Mill's ideal of many-sidedness, his practical application of what would be one of the main arguments of *On Liberty*, that 'he who knows only his own side of the case, knows little of that' (E 46).

From both Coleridge and the Saint-Simonians Mill acquired the habit of looking at past institutions and opinions in their historical context. A society's morality and its institutions formed a coherent whole, appropriate to the stage in human progress it had reached. It was facile and unhistorical to condemn a whole society for behaviour or opinions which, taken out of context, might seem barbarous or archaic. An organization now in the way of progress might once have represented the most advanced element in society. A doctrine now exploded might originally have been a great improvement on its first rivals. This view explains some of Mill's remarks which might otherwise seem odd in a sceptic and an anti-clerical, as when, reviewing some volumes of Michelet's *History of France*, he said of the Middle Ages that his own views were 'strongly Guelphic . . . almost always with the popes against the Kings' (W xiii 505).

He did not adopt a complete historical relativism, nor the conservative attitude to current political changes that normally goes with it. The recurrent pessimism in his writings which is often taken for conservatism is rather the logical consequence of his utilitarian vision. He had been taught to believe that societies improve and progress as the individuals who compose them learn to sacrifice their immediate to their long-term interests. As their outlook expands, as it were, from the immediate gratifications of the moment, to take in the larger destinies of the human race, the old intellectual and institutional obstacles to progress are simply superseded by arrangements based on the permanent interests of mankind as revealed by science. But the corollary of this highly intellectual conception of social change is that the failure of reform, the successful resistance of entrenched interests and traditional institutions, are really symptoms of men's moral and intellectual failure, occasions for lamentation and reproach at the backwardness of contemporary society. So Mill's alternations of optimism and pessimism are quite consistent with his utilitarian beliefs.

Of course his reappraisal of his heritage baffled his friends. Mill himself added to the confusion by writing in different moods. When the cause of reform was going well, as in the years 1830–2, he yielded to the euphoria around him and wrote polemically as the theorist of a party. When it was going badly he turned back to the theory, and as he had an acuter sense than anyone else on his side of its doctrinal shortcomings, and little relish for the mere party battle, what he wrote to clarify the radical philosophy often seemed to be more critical of his friends than his opponents. When he edited the *London and Westminster Review* in the 1830s he sought to make it the organ of the party he himself called the Philosophic Radicals; but it is in this journal that we find him giving vent to some of the most serious reservations about his heritage, notably the essays on Bentham and Coleridge. The policy was too subtle for his friends, and when the dispersal of the Philosophic Radicals gave him the excuse to give up the uncongenial role of party journalist, Mill was clearly relieved that he could at last concentrate on what he was best at doing—the elucidation of a coherent philosophy of politics. This was the purpose of the *System of Logic*.

3 Science and social science

The *System of Logic* was begun in the late 1820s, in Mill's period of 'practical eclecticism', and it was completed as he grew more confident that he could reformulate the empiricism in which he had been brought up, so as to meet the objections of the institutionists on the one hand and of Comte and the positivists on the other. At first he hoped it would be a reconciling book. As men's disagreements were in the last resort differences of method, he thought a book on the method of science would help on the 'alliance among the most advanced intellects and characters of the age' (W xii 78–9). This hope survives in the book's Introduction where we read that 'Logic is common ground on which the partisans of Hartley and of Reid, of Locke and of Kant, may meet and join hands' (W vii 14). But as the book progressed Mill met critics of his philosophical heritage whose attacks made him range himself more and more on the side of Hartley and Locke and, of course, of his father. The first was Macaulay, whose criticism of the *Essay on Government* made mockery both of scholastic logic and of James Mill's conception of a science of government. The final stimulus to completion was the work of William Whewell, who provided much of the first-hand descriptions of the physical sciences and their method which Mill most needed, but whom he came to see as the chief pillar of the opposite philosophy of intuitionism and the embodiment of Anglican dominance of the ancient universities (W xiii 530). From its publication in 1843 the *System of Logic* drew criticism, and in

successive editions Mill replied to his critics. The book
therefore became more committed and less conciliatory
in the course of his lifetime. By the 1850s when he wrote
his *Autobiography* he held that it had all along been meant
to combat intuitionism, 'the great intellectual support of
false doctrines and bad institutions' (W i 233). This view
is even more forcibly expressed in the writings of his last
years. In 1865 he wrote the polemical *Examination of Sir
William Hamilton's Philosophy* in which he attacked the
heresy still more vigorously, and he altered the text of
the last three editions of the *Logic* to make it more
consistent with the case against Hamilton.

The *Logic* is radical and empiricist. Mill did not use the
word 'empiricism' as we do: in his vocabulary it means
observations not guided by scientific principles. But the
word derives from the Greek word for experience, and as
Mill thought that all our knowledge is derived from
experience, he is rightly placed in the empiricist tradition
of British philosophy which runs from Locke and Hume
to Russell and A. J. Ayer. What is peculiar to Mill's
contribution to this tradition is that he tries to combine
the radical empiricism of associationist psychology with
a conception of social science based on the paradigm of
Newtonian physics. In one direction he had to maintain
that all we know is from the evidence of the senses. In
the other he sought to show that all the sciences were
progressing towards the abstract and deductive character
of classical physics.

The first part of this programme takes up the first two
books of the *Logic*. From the start we are conscious of
Mill's reliance on the psychology of his father's *Analysis*
with its wholly philosophical account of how the mind
works. Sensations are the raw material of our knowledge:
'All we can know of Matter is the sensations which it
gives us, and the order of occurrence of those sensations'

(W vii 76). This is the doctrine philosophers call phenomenalism. Mill's classic statement of it is in the *Examination of Hamilton* (Chapters 10 and 11), where he gives the famous definition of external objects as 'permanent possibilities of sensation'. But the *Logic* has the same doctrine (W vii 58).

It is an important part of the empiricist programme to deny that we can learn anything from propositions themselves, independently of the things they describe. A preliminary move is to subject 'class' names to a reductionist analysis in Bentham's manner. When we call an object by the name of a class, such as a chair, we are not describing anything essential to chairs, for it is the general name that makes them a class (W vii 175). Mill then proceeds to deal with the syllogism, denying that it is 'a means of coming to a knowledge of what we did not know before'. The stock form of the syllogism 'All men are mortal: Socrates is a man: therefore Socrates is mortal' proves nothing in itself. All the information we want (in this case about the mortality of men) lies in the major premiss. We do not, in such a case, really infer the mortality of Socrates from the major and minor premisses; our inferring ends with the major. We observe from numerous individual instances that men die, and infer men's mortality from these. So 'all inference is from particulars to particulars' (W vii 193). Mill claims that this is borne out by the fact that simple people can attain great skill in complex operations without any knowledge of syllogistic reasoning. A savage who throws his weapon unerringly to bring down his game owes his skill 'to a long series of previous experiments, the results of which he certainly never framed into any verbal theorems or rules' (W vii 189). His skill is built up by inference from particulars; and many people attain great manual dexterity without acquiring the habit of expressing what they do in general propositions.

The major premiss of a syllogism is such a general proposition, a register of inferences already made, by which we reduce our experiences to a ready shorthand. What then is the syllogism for, if it tells us nothing new? Mill insists that it has a function, that of a collateral security for the correctness of the general proposition. The syllogism is a way of storing our experiences 'in a commodious and immediately available shape' (W vii 199).

It is worth noting that Mill is too radical to allow this argument to become a prop to blind convention. The bad thing about 'general language' he says, is that inferences made on insufficient evidence become 'hardened into general maxims; and the mind cleaves to them from habit, after it has outgrown any liability to be misled by similar fallacious appearances if they were for the first time presented; but having forgotten the particulars, it does not think of revising its own former decision' (W vii 199). He was to extend this point into a general attack upon conventional moral language in *On Liberty*. In the *Logic* he merely uses it to explain how we attain certainty in science. In complicated chains of reasoning, he allows, we do seem to proceed syllogistically. Suppose we say, for instance, that no government which earnestly seeks the good of its subjects is overthrown, and so the Prussian government will remain stable. Here, says Mill, what appears to be a series of syllogisms is really a series of inductions reduced, for brevity, to 'marks'. These marks are simply summaries to aid memory. If our memories were capacious enough to order a mass of detail we could reason without general propositions, but as they are not, we use 'marks of marks'. These enable us to build, as it were, upon previous inductions, and to turn sciences originally inductive and experimental into sciences of pure reasoning. Deduction is not a mode of reasoning opposed to induction, but the culmination of it.

The opposition is not between the terms Deductive and Inductive, but between Deductive and Experimental. A science is experimental, in proportion as every new case, which presents any peculiar features, stands in need of a new set of observations and experiments—a fresh induction. It is deductive, in proportion as it can draw conclusions, respecting cases of a new kind, by processes which bring those cases under old inductions; by ascertaining that cases which cannot be observed to have the requisite marks, have, however, marks of those marks. (W vii 219)

The sciences which remained experimental were those, like chemistry, which had not discovered 'marks of marks'. Newton's explanation of planetary motion, on the other hand, was 'the greatest example which has yet occurred of the transformation, at one stroke, of a science which was still to a great degree merely experimental, into a deductive science' (W vii 220).

In what sense, then, are the wholly deductive sciences, like mathematics, considered to be true? Are they not really systems of necessary truth which owe nothing to experience or experiment? Mill saw quite clearly that to admit that they were was to concede the intuitionist case at its strongest point, and so he attacked this argument head on. He began with geometry. Whewell and the intuitionists claimed that the axioms of geometry were true because we could not conceive of their falsity. Mill retorted that they were generalizations from our experience, and that our inability to conceive of their falsity was merely due to the strength of associative habit. Propositions like 'A circle has all its radii equal' or 'Two straight lines cannot enclose a space' were inductions from the evidence of our senses. The intuitionists said that axioms in geometry were not just true in this or that instance; they were true universally and necessarily. Mill's answer was that his opponents were mistaking an acquired capacity for an intuitive perception: the laws of association showed how men came to assume that certain truths were necessary. In mathematics too the existence of necessary truths was an illusion. 'All numbers must be numbers of something: there are no such things as numbers in the abstract. Ten must mean ten bodies or ten sounds, or ten beatings of the pulse' (W vii 254). Mill concludes that the superior accuracy of these so-called 'exact sciences' derives, not from their exactly describing real objects (for there is no such thing in nature as a straight line, and numbers are not real entities) but from their providing exact inferences—a point which will recur later when we look at Mill's conception of political economy.

Mill's account of geometry and mathematics is generally regarded as the weakest part of the *Logic*. It was Mill's own godson, Bertrand Russell, who recalled that even as a boy he could not see how $2 + 2 = 4$ was a generalization from experience, nor understand how a fresh instance of it could possibly strengthen one's belief that it was true. Subsequent developments in logic and mathematics have ensured that Mill's mistakes are now scarcely discussed. Even the layman is made uneasy by the way Mill buttresses weak arguments with the archaic assumptions of associationist psychology. But these assumptions are no less prevalent in the third book of the *Logic*, in which Mill deals with induction, and this is a section of the *Logic* which receives much more respect, perhaps because his arguments have a closer family resemblance to those of modern empiricists.

Mill defines induction as 'the operation of discovering and proving general propositions' (W vii 284) and he seeks to explain this operation in phenomenalist terms, that is, by describing the causal relations implicit in general propositions not as forces in nature but as statements of expectation. We all observe regularities in nature, and when we have seen the same thing occur a few times we expect it to recur. This Mill calls 'the observation of nature, by uncultivated intellects' (W vii 312). Such intellects will mistake a small number of coincidences for a law, which will lead them to believe that, for instance, comets cause calamities. How do we distinguish between casual uniformities and true laws? Simply by experience, which tells us some uniformities are more to be relied on than others. Experience refined by art enables the cultivated to see the need to distinguish between coincidences and true laws of nature. But what are laws of nature? Mill says that they are the strongest inductions, on which the weaker ones depend. We discover causes by induction. What we call 'cause' indeed is no more than the invariable antecedent, and what we call 'effect' is no more than the invariable consequent. The task of science is to move from weak inductions, which merely recognize regularities in nature, to stronger ones which record unvarying laws. So Mill rephrases the question to read: 'What are the fewest and simplest assumptions, which being granted, the whole existing order of nature would result?' (W vii 317).

Mill's phenomenalist analysis is directed against the idea of occult agencies in nature, of effects conceived as being part of the properties of objects, as when we say thoughtlessly that coal makes or produces a hotter fire than wood. The capacity given to objects of being the causes of other effects, says Mill, 'is not a real thing existing in the objects; it is but a name for our own conviction that they will act in a particular manner when certain new circumstances arise' (W vii 337). The difficulty about this paraphrase is that it makes the attribution of cause too compendious. Mill is clearly anxious to show that our understanding of the world around us need not be a difficult or recondite matter, which perhaps accounts for his mixing examples from social life and the natural world as if to convey that the ways we understand each do not differ in kind. But in both social and physical science we need to distinguish, in the welter of antecedent conditions of an event, between those which were essential and those which were incidental in its production. In fact, we need to know what were the *necessary* and what the *sufficient* conditions of an event. Mill's idea of cause is stretched to cover all antecedent conditions, and it comes to look too cumbersome for explanations of human affairs, and too loose and general for explanations of physical events.

When we say that a man died because he ate a particular dish, Mill insists that we are speaking incorrectly, by designating one cause as the precipitant one; whereas we should give *all* the antecedents, including the facts of his constitution, his state of health, perhaps even of the weather. For our analysis of cause to be correct, our enumeration of the antecedents must be complete; and though in everyday explanations we do often single out a particular factor as the efficient cause, this is an illusion. It is like saying that the decision of an assembly was *caused* by the chairman's casting vote. Nobody could seriously claim that this was really the cause of the assembly's decision: it was merely the last condition which preceded the decision. What we call the cause of an event, Mill argues, is actually more complex; it is 'the sum total of the conditions, positive and negative, taken together; the whole of the contingencies of every description, which being realized, the consequent invariably follows' (W vii 332).

But as far as human behaviour goes, does not our habit of isolating one factor as more important than another mean rather more than Mill allows? In his example, the chairman's casting vote is not the sole cause of the assembly's decision, but it is undeniably more crucial in producing it than any previous vote on either side. What makes us more interested in it than the others is that it carries a heavier load of responsibility. We might think the chairman more responsible *by definition* than any other member, so that his abstention from voting was a graver abdication of responsibility than any of theirs, if only because it must have come after previous votes had clarified the issues. A full explanation of the assembly's decision, in other words, would have to discriminate between them: it could never be the same as a complete enumeration of causes. Mill's doctrine that we have no other notion of cause than that of antecedents and consequents is implausible, because it seems to have no room for human motive, and seems to minimize individual will.

Mill was aware of the strength of the intuitionists' case for the will, which he sets out very fairly. They claimed that our knowledge of our own wills was independent of experience, and so constituted knowledge a priori. On the contrary, says Mill, will is simply a physical cause like any other.

> Our will causes our bodily actions in the same sense, and in no other, in which cold causes ice, or a spark causes an explosion of gunpowder. The volition, a state of our mind, is the antecedent; the motion of our limbs in conformity to the volition, is the consequent. This sequence I conceive to be not a subject of direct consciousness . . . (W vii 355)

Mill's main target here is what he calls the 'original fetishism', by which primitive people extend the notion of agency to the non-sentient objects around them, a tendency which gives way as our knowledge of phenomena extends, and we realize that our own bodily and mental structures do not offer exceptions to the laws around us. As a caution against superstition this is very laudable, but Mill is so determined to prove the intuitionist wrong, that he deprives himself of any alternative account of individual identity. An individual for him is nothing more than the sum of the psychological events which compose a particular mind; he has no other way of describing a person than as a locus of sensations. What gives anyone the right to suppose he has experiences, thought, and expectations peculiar to himself, Mill cannot explain. He was in his later work to develop an acute, even frantic, sense of the threats which social developments posed to the individual, but his own associationist heritage tended to the belief that the environment was everything and the individual nothing.

If Mill's account of causation in human affairs seems unduly ungenerous to the individual will, when he looks at natural processes he seems equally hampered by his psychological assumptions. He sees that to explain the causes of phenomena something stronger is needed than invariable sequence. Night invariably follows day, but that does not make day the cause of night. So he tries to offer a definition of cause which will go beyond invariable sequence yet stop short of occult agency. He sees that in any explanation of a physical event, we need to know which were the decisive and which the incidental factors. In his own example of the man who dies from food-poisoning, we want to know which food killed him rather more urgently than what was his general state of health. If we know it was a poisonous mushroom, we can help prevent similar deaths, but if we are supposed to enumerate all the factors contributing to that one death, we shall get nowhere. We need a distinction between necessary and sufficient causes; but, for reasons we shall come to, Mill disliked the word necessary, which he insisted only meant 'unconditionalness'. So he finally defined cause as 'the antecedent, or the concurrence of antecedents, on which [a phenomenon] is invariably and *unconditionally* consequent' (W vii 340).

On the whole Mill's critics have held that he equated cause with sufficient conditions, and that this is plausible when applied to the sort of explanations we make in everyday life when our own observation is all we have to go on but is too imprecise for natural science, where a more rigorous elimination and selection of the antecedents is supposed to lay bare the causal mechanisms behind phenomena. It is not merely that Mill seems to be asking us to translate the language of cause and effect into the more artificial language of sensations, but also that, as he himself admits, 'mere constancy of succession' does not seem 'a sufficiently stringent bond of union for so peculiar a relation as that of cause and effect' (W viii 837). It seems easier to conceive of 'forces in nature' than 'contingent future facts'.

Mill thought that by providing a careful tabulation of methods of induction he could fix the difference between truly scientific laws and merely empirical ones. He gives the four methods in Chapter 8 of Book III. They are the Method of Agreement, the Method of Difference, the Method of Residues and the Method of Concomitant Variations. The first two in combination are sometimes taken to make a fifth. There is no need here for an elaborate analysis of these. They amount to rules for the elimination of extraneous factors in a situation so as to assign causes, and we do actually use them in everyday life. When I want to find out why all but one of my roses are flourishing, I use the Method of Agreement; when I want to find out why my car won't start, the Method of Difference, and so on. But are these the methods actually used by the physical scientist to discover causal laws?

Mill's opponent Whewell said they were not, and modern discussion has tended to uphold him. Mill's view of the mind as an essentially passive receptacle of sensations implies that our knowledge of nature's laws is built up 'by successive steps of generalization from experience'. The emphasis is on the facts encountering the mind rather than the mind engaging with the facts. Regularities in nature suggest themselves. Whewell however held that we had to start with a theory first, for without it we could not see that they were regularities. We probed nature with a series of questions each embodying a hypothesis. There was 'a mask of theory over the whole face of nature'. To Mill this was too haphazard. He called a hypothesis 'a mere supposition', and said of Whewell's method that it recognized 'absolutely no mode of induction except that of trying hypothesis after hypothesis until one is found which fits the phenomena' (W vii 490, 503).

The modern case against Mill's type of inductivism has been mainly associated with Karl Popper, but it goes back to Hume. Hume had pointed out that, however many times we observe that A is followed by B, we have no logical warrant to suppose B will *always* follow A. That we expect it to is a fact of our psychological make-up, not a matter of logical entailment. Popper has added a further claim. Many recurrent instances of a phenomenon are not enough to verify a general statement, but one contrary instance is enough to falsify it. Any number of instances of white swans cannot prove the truth of the statement 'All swans are white', but one black swan is enough to disprove it. So there is an asymmetry between verification and falsification, and as scientific proof cannot rest on the former, it must rest on the latter. Empirical evidence cannot verify a theory (though it may strengthen a conjecture or hypothesis); it can only falsify it. It follows that induction cannot build up a body of certain, empirically verified knowledge, and that the business of forming hypotheses is a central task of the scientific observer, and not, as Mill supposed, a mere form of guesswork. In short, Whewell was on the right lines. Scientific advance is concerned with intuition and imagination, and the war Mill envisaged between them and empiricism rests on a false antithesis.

Mill's view of the physical sciences was clouded by his commitment to associationist psychology and the extreme empiricism which it entailed. When he considered the science of society he had to reconcile this empiricism with a wholly deductive approach. Utilitarianism claimed to deduce its conclusions from the facts of human nature, but it was a human nature conceived as it were in a historical void, as a residuum of qualities independent of space and time. How could a science of society be deduced from data no one had proved?

Mill first met this problem in Macaulay's attack upon his father's *Essay on Government*. James Mill assumed a few principles of human nature, and deduced a whole science from them, passing over as ambiguous and unreliable the lessons to be derived from actual historical examples. The result, Macaulay said, was 'an elaborate treatise on Government, from which, but for two or three passing allusions, it would not appear that the author was aware that any governments actually existed among men'. The older Mill's method was a regression to the syllogistic logic of the Middle Ages, which had long since been discredited in the learned world by the experimental method advocated by Bacon. To found a true science of politics on experimental principles, on the method of induction, we must, Macaulay insisted, proceed 'by generalizing with judgment and diffidence,—by perpetually bringing the theory which we have constructed to the test of new facts,—by correcting, or rather altogether abandoning it, according as those new facts prove it to be partially or fundamentally unsound'.

This advice is impeccably empiricist and Mill might have

been expected to agree with it. But he rejected it. In the *Autobiography* he is severe on Macaulay's idea of a social science. 'I saw . . . that he stood up for the empirical mode of treating political phenomena, against the philosophical [that is, scientific]; that even in physical science, his notion of philosophizing might have recognized Kepler, but would have excluded Newton and Laplace' (W i 165). This comment is of course a résumé of the argument in the *Logic*, that sciences begin as experimental and advance to becoming systems of pure deductive reasoning. In Book III there is a clear rebuke to Macaulay for invoking the authority of Bacon (W vii 482). Macaulay's point, however, was not about how the sciences had evolved, but about whether the first principles of a science of politics were or were not derived from experience. How did James Mill arrive at the principles of human nature from which his science was deduced? Obviously by experience. But was that experience of human nature in politics or out of it?

> If it includes experience of the manner in which men act when intrusted with the powers of government, then those principles of human nature from which the science of government is to be deduced, can only be known after going through that inductive process by which we propose to arrive at the science of government.

In that case the study of politics would have to come before principles of human nature, and the latter would depend on the former. But John Mill was determined not to admit the case for empiricism even in an infant science of politics. The reason was that he could not afford to allow that Macaulay was right, without seriously damaging political economy; and he defended political economy not because it was a mature science (utilitarians liked to flaunt the fact that it was very new) but because it was abstract and deductive in its reasoning, like Newtonian physics.

This becomes clear from his first formal defence of his father's a priori method—an essay, written in 1831 but not published till late 1836, 'On the Definition of Political Economy'. Mill's strategy is to shift the defence of the method from a science of politics, where it was weak, to political economy, from which we saw it had originally been borrowed, and for which a Whig like Macaulay might have more respect. The whole drift of this essay (which anticipates the *Logic*'s last book) is to deny the worth of empiricism in the moral or, as we would say, the social sciences.

Mill begins with the distinction already touched on, between science and art. 'Science is a collection of *truths*; art a body of *rules*, or directions for conduct' (W iv 312). So Adam Smith's definition of political economy as the science by which a nation is made rich, is actually a confusion of art and science. The strictly scientific part consists of 'the laws which regulate the production, distribution and consumption of wealth' (313). The art of becoming rich stands to these laws as the art of gunnery stands to the science of ballistics. To mark the boundary between the science of political economy and those sciences like botany, physiology, and metallurgy which are related to it, Mill draws another distinction, between physical and moral science. The former concerns the laws of matter; the latter those of mind. Few physical sciences depend on the moral sciences, but all the moral ones presuppose the physical. In the production of corn, for instance, there are many laws of matter (regulating the germination of seed, the climate, and so on) and one law of mind, 'that man desires to possess subsistence, and consequently wills the necessary means of procuring it' (317). Political economy differs from the physical sciences in involving laws of the human mind. So Mill completes his definition of it as 'the science which treats of the

65

production and distribution of wealth, so far as they depend upon the laws of human nature' (318). He is careful to separate it from ethics, which is an art, not a science (319–20). It is also distinct from the laws relating to man as a social being, which are the province of 'social economy, speculative politics, or the natural history of society'. Political economy deals with man 'solely as a being who desires to possess wealth'. Not that the political economist thinks men really are merely acquisitive beings, but simply 'because this is the mode in which science must necessarily proceed' (322). Its method must be a priori: 'It reasons, and . . . must necessarily reason, from assumptions, not from facts. It is built upon hypotheses, strictly analogous to those which, under the name of definitions, are the foundation of the other abstract sciences' (325–6). In the moral sciences, unlike the physical, there is no room for laboratory experiment. You cannot for instance experiment to decide whether or not a policy of agricultural protection makes a nation prosperous. So political economy is a deductive science, its scientific character lying in the accuracy of its deductions from the abstraction of economic man. Mill does have a role for empirical verification or confirmation a posteriori, but it is not large, because economic laws are not strictly predictive and therefore are not strictly verifiable. When we meet 'a discrepancy between our anticipations and the actual fact' (Mill does not say 'between our predictions and the actual event') it is because economic laws are subject to 'disturbing causes' which operate 'like friction in mechanics' (330, 332). For this reason we can only talk of tendencies: economic prediction is not a matter of saying what *will* occur, but rather of describing 'a power acting with a certain intensity in that direction' (337). But because the disturbing causes are so complex, there can be no sure way of verifying the laws.

The admission that political economy dealt only with a limited area of human activity made the elaboration of a general science of society all the more urgent, if the universality of scientific method was to be upheld. It was the promise of such a general science of society which drew Mill to Comte, whose enterprise he once called 'very nearly the grandest work of the age'. Yet his reception of Comte's philosophy only throws into relief his greater debt to Ricardo and his father. Even the political disagreement which led Mill eventually to declare that Comte aspired to 'a despotism of society over the individual, surpassing anything contemplated in the political ideal of the most rigid disciplinarian among the ancient philosophers' (E 19–20) had its roots deep in Mill's youth. No one as familiar as Mill was with Bentham's fantasies of central control could have contemplated Comte's system with complete surprise.

It is sometimes said that Mill adopted Comte's 'law of three stages', according to which societies go through three successive states, each with its specific mental attitude and the institutions appropriate to it. Mill did adopt this classification; but it was after all only a neater and more comprehensive solution to a problem which he had first met in his father's *History of British India*, and continued to confront in his work at the India House. Any utilitarian approach to human morality is vulnerable to the objection that different societies have different conceptions of what constitutes good or bad conduct. The Hindus thought it right to burn widows on the funeral pyres of their husbands. The British thought the custom barbarous and tried to stamp it out. James Mill's solution to this diversity of moral values was to say that, if you set societies on a scale of progress, it became clear that the measure of their advance was the degree to which they made utility the standard of conduct. It was his solemn application of this crude yardstick to Indian culture which makes his *History* a classic in the history of philistinism. He was unable to see, or at least to admit, that there could be different levels of achievement *within* a given society. Degrading religious superstition might coexist with art, sculpture, and building of great merit; great intellectual feats might be compatible with technological backwardness. James Mill used a two-edged argument to prove all Hindu achievements were on the same low level. If their morals were low, he said it was proof of their barbarism; but if their poetry and literature were remarkable, he said these attainments were not essential to civilization. The method did imply some account of how the different attainments which make up civilization evolve, but it was crude and incomplete. Comte's classification was more sophisticated, and explained within a historical framework how mathematics, astronomy, physics, chemistry, and biology had in turn become positive sciences, as they became more complex and more concrete. Most concrete of all, and the culmination of the process, was sociology, the science of man in society.

Obviously Comte's work helped Mill bring together his reflections on the nature of scientific proof with his wider quest for a scientific foundation for politics. But Comte thought his system could lead to a reordering of society straight away, without too much regard for dissenting opinions. Mill thought of sociology as a larger, more general science, embracing more specific sciences like political economy and jurisprudence; and whereas Comte assumed his positive polity rendered these sciences obsolete, Mill insisted that they provided the methodological discipline without which the larger science of society could never be more than vague speculation. Beneath this difference of expectations there were more fundamental differences of principle.

They disagreed about the role of the individual in the new science. Comte thought that a positive social science would improve on its 'metaphysical' forebears in studying the actions of men from the outside, as one might a species of animals. 'Il ne faut pas expliquer l'humanité par l'homme, mais au contraire l'homme par l'humanité.' Comte omitted psychology altogether from his scheme of sciences, and dismissed political economy as metaphysical, the characteristic expression of lawyers and literary men who would be useless in any positive reordering of society. Mill however had always insisted on starting with the individual and the laws of his being. In his first brush with the positivist faith in the 1820s he had asked of the Saint-Simonians' conception of the *pouvoir spirituel* whether it meant anything other than 'the insensible influence of mind over mind' (W xii 41). In the *Logic* he elaborated this. 'The laws of the phenomena of society are, and can be, nothing but the laws of the actions and passions of human beings united in the social state' (W viii 879).

Mill and Comte also differed on the nature of the laws which governed the individual. Comte thought that the laws of mind would be found through anatomy and physiology, and he was particularly struck by the theories of the German phrenologist Franz Joseph Gall (1758–1828). Mill was suspicious of phrenology with its deterministic implications, and in any case the science of mind as he conceived it was 'more advanced than the portion of physiology which corresponds to it' (W viii 851). Least of all could he swallow Comte's claim that as women had smaller brains than men, they were naturally inferior, or his conclusion that society under the positivist dispensation would forbid divorce. Of course in theory associationism should have been as deterministic as classical physics. Sensations were to Mill's science of mind what atoms were in physics; association playing the role in mental phenomena which attraction plays in physical. Any human science really modelled on the physical sciences must elucidate rigorous, predictive laws, from which no individual could claim exemption. Mill certainly saw the point of Comte's claim that, as there was no such thing as the freedom to disagree with the laws of astronomy, so it would be absurd to allow dissent from the laws of a positive science of society once they were established. But he had strong personal reasons for rejecting this argument.

During the crisis of 1826 he had been oppressed by the deterministic implications of associationism, by the thought that he might be 'the helpless slave of antecedent circumstances' (W i 175). On his recovery he needed to believe that one may use a knowledge of the laws of association to alter one's own character. In the last book of the *Logic* he asks whether the actions of human beings are 'subject to invariable laws'. (It is interesting that he puts the argument for necessity, or, as we would say, determinism, into the mouth of a follower of Robert Owen. In fact it was an argument advanced by James Mill.) He first defines 'necessity' as the doctrine 'that, given the motives which are present to an individual's mind, and given likewise the character and disposition of the individual, the manner in which he will act might be unerringly inferred' (W viii 837). If we knew all the circumstances, we could foretell a man's conduct as surely as we can predict any physical event. Put thus, says Mill, the doctrine is unobjectionable, for we do not in fact resent it when people we know well predict our behaviour: we should conclude they thought poorly of us if they could not do so. But many people, he admits, mean more by 'necessity' than this. They confuse it with fatalism. Instead of taking cause to mean 'invariable, certain, and unconditional sequence', they think it means 'some peculiar tie, or mysterious constraint'. They believe 'not only that what is about to happen, will be the infallible result of the causes which produce it . . . but moreover that there is no use in struggling against it; that it will happen however we may strive to prevent it' (840). This is clearly the view which had distressed him in 1826. His mature refutation of it is that, though our actions are indeed formed by circumstances, we can nevertheless alter the circumstances.

> We cannot, indeed, directly will to be different from what we are. But neither did those who are supposed to have formed our characters, directly will that we should be what we are. Their will had no direct power except over their own actions. They made us what they did make us, by willing, not the end, but the requisite means; and we, when our habits are not too inveterate, can, by similarly willing the requisite means, make ourselves different. If they could place us under the influence of certain circumstances, we, in like manner, can place ourselves under the influence of other circumstances. We are exactly as capable of making our own character, *if we will*, as others are of making it for us (840).

The language strongly suggests a sort of usurpation of his father's role. He adds, still more autobiographically, that the very fact of regretting the influences which have formed our characters belies the doctrine of fatalism, because 'A person who does not wish to alter his character, cannot be the person who is supposed to feel discouraged or paralysed by thinking himself unable to do it.' Moral freedom *is* the wish to alter our characters, and as virtuous action is action by conscious choice, this confirms the old adage that only the virtuous man is free.

If then we can alter our environment as we wish, what

need have we of social science? That should tell us how society is developing and why; but if we have power to interfere with the process, it can never never be an accurate or precisely predictive science. Mill's answer is to sketch a new science, which he calls 'Ethology', which would propound the laws of the formation of character, and would serve as a bridge between psychology and sociology.

> If ... we employ the name Psychology for the science of the elementary laws of mind, Ethology will serve for the ulterior science which determines the kind of character produced in conformity to those general laws, by any set of circumstances, physical or moral. According to this definition, Ethology is the science which corresponds to the art of education; in the widest sense of the term, including the formulation of national or collective character as well as individual (869).

He calls it 'the Exact Science of Human Nature', but he does not say its laws will make possible reliable predictions, only that they will 'affirm tendencies'. Like political economy, its method is 'altogether deductive' (870). Of course its laws would not attain the predictive accuracy of astronomy 'for thousands of years to come', but that delay would be due not to the complexity of the laws but to the complexity of the data to which they are applied. In any case, 'an amount of knowledge quite insufficient for prediction, may be most valuable for guidance' (878).

Was this a *rapprochement* with Macaulay? If it was, Mill would not admit it. He calls Macaulay's conception of a science of politics a misunderstanding of 'the Chemical Method', a vulgar Baconianism typical of 'practitioners in politics, who rather employ the commonplaces of philosophy to justify their practice, than seek to guide their practice by philosophic principles' (887). His father's method he calls 'the Geometrical or Abstract Method', and he is very anxious to be kind about it. Though the 'interest philosophy of the Bentham school' erred in having too narrow a conception of human motive, this was at least an error 'peculiar to thinking and studious minds'. But he adds that these minds made the mistake of presenting 'as the scientific treatment of a great philosophical question what should have passed for the mere polemics of the day' (892–3). In other words, the *Essay in Government* was only a political pamphlet.

But having thrown out the evidence of history as Macaulay invoked it, Mill readmits it in the form of Comte's 'inverse deductive method'. He has all along insisted that a social science, whether political economy, or ethology, or sociology, must derive its laws from the laws of mind, that its accuracy must lie in the correctness of its deductions, and that the difficulty of prediction in such human sciences lies not in the complexity of the laws themselves but in the computation of their effects. It is hard enough to calculate the effects of two or three converging laws in physics; it is almost impossibly difficult to do so in sociology. The actions of individuals being governed by psychological and ethological laws (Mill is assuming the new science will provide them) we can know the social effects they *tend* to produce. The complex part is compounding the effects of many tendencies and coexisting causes, and this will be beyond human capacity. But, says Mill, there is hope. We can use the method of Verification to check the result. This inverts the usual inductive process as he has described it.

> Instead of deducing our conclusions by reasoning, and verifying them by observation, we in some cases begin by obtaining them provisionally from specific experience, and afterwards connect them with the

73

principles of human nature by *à priori* reasonings, which reasonings are thus a real Verification. (897)

What this means becomes clear from an example further on, when Mill discusses the phenomenon of social progress. If we ask if there is one element in social man which predominates over others as 'the agent of social movement' we find, by 'a striking instance of consilience', that the evidence of history and the facts of human nature agree. Both show that this element is 'the state of the speculative faculties of mankind'. We know from human nature that a desire for greater material comfort is the impulse behind improvements in the arts of life. We know from history that great social changes have been produced by changes in opinion and modes of thought. The two together amounted to proof. So Comte's law of three stages seemed to Mill to have 'that high degree of scientific evidence, which is derived from the concurrence of the indications of history with the probabilities derived from the constitution of the human mind' (928).

Mill's confidence that the determinant of social progress is the state of the speculative faculties of men may seem so typical of Victorian liberal optimism as to make his differences with Macaulay seem relatively insignificant. But they are fundamental. He may have admitted that Macaulay was right in saying that James Mill's science of government was drawn from too narrow a conception of human nature, but he never admitted that the general procedure was faulty: *some* conception of human nature, resting on the fundamental laws of mind, remained for him an indispensable preliminary for any social science. To give that up was to weaken fatally the twin supports of his creed, associationism and political economy. He was prepared to take from Comte a philosophy of history which he failed to acknowledge in Macaulay or his antecedents, but even

Comte's historicism had to be tried by the prior laws of mind. As he grew older Mill tended to put the emphasis more on the laws of mind than the evidence of history. In 1865 in his final estimate of Comte he declared that if a sociological theory based on historical evidence contradicts the laws of human nature 'we may know that history has been misinterpreted and that the theory is false' (W x 307).

This cramping loyalty to his inherited methodology accounts for the disappearance from Mill's later writings of that sense of the past which marks some of his earlier historical essays. His early ambition to write a history of the French Revolution, his enthusiasm for Carlyle's imaginative evocations of past societies, his eager response to the work of Michelet, are in the end displaced by the rigid schema of Comte's law of three stages and his own gloss upon it. That effectively meant confining his historical interest to those ages in which the 'progressive mind' seemed to anticipate his own values: fifth-century Athens, pre-Christian Rome, the Protestant Reformation, and the French Enlightenment. Macaulay's optimism drew upon a rich and varied conception of a political tradition, and was expressed in a joyous appreciation of the material and moral improvements going on around him. Mill's appreciation of his age was by contrast so severely limited by his philosophical principles, his expectations of his contemporaries were so screwed up to his own pitch of high-minded virtue, that he was much more disposed to note decline than improvement.

4 Political economy

After the breach with Comte, Mill came to feel that a proper sociology lay so far in the future that his own efforts were best employed in expanding the traditional doctrines in such a way as to meet the objections aimed at its first practitioners. He later said that he wrote the *Principles of Political Economy* 'to rescue from the hands of such people the truths they misapply, and by combining these with other truths to which they are strangers, to deduce conclusions capable of being of some use to the progress of mankind' (W xiv 37). He wrote it rapidly, beginning late in 1846, and completing the first draft by March 1847. It is consistently lucid, sometimes vivid, and its argument has little of the strained quality of some parts of the *Logic*. In the *Logic* Mill was a lonely pioneer, except at the beginning, and the fact that he owed so much to an antagonist, Whewell, suggests that few people in his immediate circle were competent to follow or to criticize his arguments. But in the *Principles* he was summarizing a body of economic writing with which he had been familiar from his childhood, and which already contained a good deal of high-quality writing dissenting from the main orthodoxy of Smith and Ricardo. So he was in his element. He was a born teacher, who excelled at making difficult and intractable subjects plain to the ordinary reader, and the *Principles* is, among other things, an excellent textbook, possibly the best place to begin a study of Ricardian economics. Its success was immediate. It did what James Mill's *Elements*, and the dramatized lessons of the 'useful knowledge' school failed to do; it popularized political economy and removed the stigma of 'the dismal science'.

This did not mean any concessions of importance to Comte's theories. The *Principles* is a very Ricardian book, and was meant to be. On the eve of its publication Mill told a friend that he doubted if there would be 'a single opinion (on pure political economy) in the book, which may not be exhibited as a corollary from his [Ricardo's] doctrines' (W xiii 731). Critics have reacted to this fidelity on Mill's part in different ways. Some are disappointed at Mill's failure to add anything significant to the basic theory he had imbibed in the 1820s, chiding him, for example, for the complacent remark on the theory of Value: 'Happily, there is nothing in the laws of Value which remains for the present or any future writer to clear up; the theory of the subject is complete' (W iii 456). Others have said that Mill failed to bring the theory up to date with developments in his lifetime; that though his book appeared thirty years after Ricardo's and went through seven editions before his death, during which time the predictions Ricardo had made were all falsified, Mill still stuck to the original scheme he had been taught. There is a vast and technical literature on Mill's economic theory. Here we need only note that, if what has been said already about Mill's conception of social science is right, neither charge is fair to Mill's intentions in the book. He thought the accuracy of political economy lay in its deductions from assumed premises, and its predictions were strictly conditional on the individual's choice. The laws of economics were not to be blindly obeyed, but intelligently used. If a man chose to act in a certain way, he must expect certain results; if he struck for higher wages, his real wages would decline, and so on. Political economy presupposed an individual willing to use the deductions of the science to help him understand his condition and improve his lot. It was not a predictive science so much as a logic of choice; for individuals in its smaller details, for governments in its larger prescriptions.

These assumptions make the *Principles* fundamentally at odds with the *dirigisme* of Comte, and even with the sort of interventionism made in the name of public utility which one might expect from a disciple of Bentham. It illustrates the point made earlier, that liberal individualism owes more to Ricardo's political economy than to Bentham's ethics and jurisprudence. We may note three ways in which Mill's liberalism is shaped by his allegiance to Ricardian economics. First, in trying to make Ricardo's system more congenial to the ordinary reader, he makes it much less deterministic. Secondly, he on the whole preferred *laissez-faire* as a principle to State intervention in matters of economic and social policy. Finally, even his qualified approval of socialism was made in the context of a free-market system.

Undoubtedly, Ricardo's 'strong cases', and his aversion to actual examples, gave his system its air of inexorable gloom. It made popular radicals like Cobbett and romantic Tories like Southey claim that the political economists were merely cold-hearted calculators of human suffering. John Mill was torn between upholding the scientific pretensions of his teachers and denying their inhumane implications. Partly it was a question of style. He saw that Ricardo and his father had 'trusted too much to the intelligibleness of the abstract, when not embodied in the concrete', and that if their formulations were set out with historical evidence and illustrative detail, they could be made much more acceptable. But Mill also altered the character of the Ricardian laws. In Book I he deals with the laws of Production, in Book II with those of Distribution. The former he says 'partake of the character of physical truths. There is nothing optional or arbitrary about them.' But Distribution is 'a matter of human institution solely.

The things once there, mankind, individually or collectively, can do with them what they like' (W ii 199). The distinction has been criticized as too rigid. In practice Mill did not apply it very stringently. In his exposition the Ricardian laws appear as tendencies, allowing of different responses according to situation. Few people believed more firmly than he did in the Malthusian law of population, for instance; but on the same page he can say *both* that improvements in the conditions of the labouring classes can rarely 'do anything more than give a temporary margin, speedily filled up by an increase of their numbers', *and* that England had seen steady increases in subsistence and employment along with smaller proportional increases in the population (W ii 159). In other words, the Malthusian law survives in the weaker form of a tendency, more or less prevalent according to the level of education in a given community.

He also blurred the stark contrasts between the three classes in Ricardo's system. The chief target is no longer the landowner idly receiving a steady increase of rent, while the capitalist faces diminishing returns and the labourer staggers along at a bare level of subsistence. Mill is as hostile to idleness and luxury as his father (in practice, perhaps more so), but it is the conspicuous consumption of the new-rich middle classes which he attacks, quite as much as the old landed aristocracy. In fact, because Mill is concerned to flesh out and clothe the Ricardian skeleton, and for this drew on his own observation and experience, the ordinary reader is made more aware of bourgeois vanity than of landowning arrogance. The landowner as such is no longer the enemy. The small landed proprietor comes in for a good deal of praise, perhaps because Mill had learned from Tocqueville about his importance in American democracy. The labourer's improvidence is still a threat to his living standards, but he is plainly seen to be winning the battle against the law of diminishing returns, because he benefits from every improvement in the 'arts of production' which tends to cheapen manufactured goods. His food may cost more, but other goods will cost less (W ii 184–5).

In all this, Mill's tone is more optimistic than Ricardo's. Even the stationary state which for Ricardo (though not for James Mill) was an imminent horror, as wages rose to provide for increased numbers and investment flagged, becomes in Mill a prospect to be positively welcomed. He could see no pleasure in expansion for its own sake. Increased production might be an important aim for poor countries, but for advanced ones a better distribution of existing wealth was more important still. For Mill, a happy society consists of

> a well-paid and affluent body of labourers; no enormous fortunes, except what were earned and accumulated during a single lifetime; but a much larger body of persons than at present, not only exempt from the coarser toils, but with sufficient leisure, both physical and mental, from mechanical details, to cultivate freely the graces of life, and afford examples of them to the classes less favourably circumstanced for their growth. (W iii 755)

The image of an orderly classroom in which the older children help the younger is never far from Mill's vision of the future. He was not excited by the thought of a world spinning down the ringing grooves of change. On the contrary, he wanted a world in which one could still commune with nature in solitude, and he saw that world under threat. In his youth he had picked wild flowers in country lanes which in his middle age became London streets, and he thought there would be no satisfaction in contemplating the world with nothing left to the spontaneous activity of nature; with every rood of land brought into cultivation, which is capable of growing food for human beings; every flowery waste or natural pasture ploughed up, all quadrupeds or birds which are not domesticated for man's use exterminated as his rivals for food, every hedgerow or superfluous tree rooted out, and scarcely a place left where a wild shrub or flower could grow without being eradicated as a weed in the name of improved agriculture. (W iii 756)

If that was what industrialism cost, then we would all gain if industrialism ground to a halt. The stationary state in Mill's work becomes a way of fusing the inexorable laws of the political economists with the cult of nature in romantic poetry, making the former seem less callous and the latter more useful.

Mill was consistently liberal in the powers he was willing to grant the State. In the light of his views on the distribution of wealth this is worth noticing. A utilitarian might be expected to want to use the powers of government to overrule individual or sectional interests for the sake of the greatest happiness of the greatest number. Mill hints at something like this when he says that 'the ends of government are as comprehensive as those of the social union', and consist of 'all the good, and all the immunity from evil, which the existence of government can be made either directly or indirectly to bestow' (807). But when he considers in detail particular functions of the State, Mill is much more concerned to protect individual enterprise and initiative from State encroachment.

In the field of taxation, for instance, he shows a characteristic dislike of the prodigal spending of wealth. But when he considers a graduated property tax (that is, an income tax on which larger incomes pay a higher percentage) he is worried that the aim of equalizing wealth may tend to 'relieve the prodigal at the expense of the prudent'. 'To tax the larger incomes at a higher percentage than the smaller, is to lay a tax on industry and economy; to impose a penalty on people for having worked harder and saved more than their neighbours' (810–11). So he advocates taxing inheritances above a certain amount. 'No one person should be permitted to acquire, by inheritance, more than the amount of a moderate independence' (887). In cases of intestacy, the property should escheat to the State, after an adequate provision for descendants. Mill was against taxing income from investments, because this would harm those who could not work, and for whose security the provision had been originally made. He thought the current rate of income tax of 7d. in the pound involved an injustice, in that it took the same from the salary-earner as from the man who lived off his investments, and restricted the savings of the former. Here his argument actually favours the rich. He disliked a tax which fell both on income and on savings. But since the rich have most to save, exempting savings from taxation benefits them most. Mill defended this apparent partiality with the argument that the rich enjoy the advantage 'only in proportion as they abdicate the personal use of their riches', and prefer productive investments by which wealth is 'distributed in wages among the poor' (816). The thrifty and accumulating bourgeoisie in Mill's scheme therefore escape heavy taxation in so far as they refrain from conspicuous extravagance. But something of the old hostility to the landed aristocracy survives in Mill's proposals to tax increases in rent from land. The landlords, he says, 'grow richer, as it were in their sleep, without working, risking, or economizing' (819–20). For the same general reasons he was against primogeniture; and to McCulloch's argument for the great landed estates, that they were a standing incentive to 'the ingenuity and enterprise of the other classes', Mill replies primly that people are more stimulated 'by the example of somebody who has earned a fortune, than by the mere sight of somebody who possesses one' (890).

Mill's concern to protect wealth energetically and conscientiously earned leads naturally to a fairly modest conception of what government can do to advance the welfare of its subjects. He shared the view of his teachers that governments, even in modern times, had been too anxious to interfere in the working of the economy and that their interference had been generally harmful. But in his youth he had assumed that these faults were characteristic of undemocratic governments, and that as a government really representing a majority of the people could have no interest at variance with the general interest, the reasons for opposing government intervention would diminish as democracy advanced. By the time he wrote the *Principles* he was more disillusioned. Experience, he says, shows that popular governments (and here he seems to have been influenced by Tocqueville's picture of the United States) are no less ready than oligarchical ones to encroach on private life, and the tendency in modern society for masses to prevail over individuals made it particularly urgent to protect that 'originality of mind and individuality of character' on which human progress depended (939–40).

He therefore criticized the sort of bureaucratic control Bentham had dreamed of and Comte brought so much nearer reality. His objection to Continental governments (which Bentham would hardly have considered a criticism) was that 'six or eight men, living at the capital and known by the name of ministers, demand that the whole public business of the country shall pass, or be supposed to pass under their individual eye' and that this meant the overruling of local interests and peculiarities. Mill wanted local administrators to have more share in initiating policy, and he thought that, though central government might be made more efficient, it was still true that individuals did things which affected themselves better than governments could (941). Above all, central government, by drawing talent to itself, was liable to inhibit what Mill calls the active energies of a people, 'labour, contrivance, judgment, self-control' (943). Even the central government of a democracy therefore would not be able to obviate the need for strong local institutions.

Mill concludes that the general rule should be *laissez-faire*: 'every departure from it, unless required by some great good, is a certain evil'. The exceptions to the rule were education, the care of children and the insane, planned colonization, poor relief, some public utilities such as water, and the regulation of hours of labour. Obviously the first of these, being bound up with maintaining the active energies of a people, interested him most, and he justified the departure from *laissez-faire* and the rule that the consumer is the best judge, with the argument that children are not competent judges. 'The uncultivated cannot be competent judges of cultivation' (947). A society has the right to provide for its own future and as the poor generally will not or cannot pay, government must. This is not to cosset the poor or encourage idleness, for education is 'help towards doing without help' (949). Moreover, government should confine itself to requiring some instruction, not specify what sort of instruction it should be. In a similar spirit Mill approved of the 'workhouse test' of the 1834 Poor Law. The State was not in a position to judge who deserved help and who did not; all it could ensure was that no one starved.

It may seem odd that Mill should have laid such stress on the principle that each individual is the best judge of his own interests, yet at the same time have written favourably of trade unions and even declared himself a socialist. The contradiction is explained partly by his puritanical dislike of mere accumulation, which we have seen led him to welcome the stationary state; and partly by his amiable habit of throwing his authority behind an unpopular cause in order to prevent too easy a victory to the opposite side. He did not have much experience of working-class life, nor any natural sympathy with the poor, being too concerned that they conform to his preconceptions about moral improvement for his comments on their conditions to have much warmth or vividness. The society he looked forward to was not a socialist one in the sense entertained by contemporaries like the French Socialists Louis Blanc or Pierre Joseph Proudhon. He had no plans for the abolition of property or its equalization. Rather his hope was for a general *embourgeoisement*, with everybody working for a living, enjoying a decent competence, and having leisure enough to improve his mind.

So his view of trade unions and their role is quite compatible with the free play of market forces. He was (like his teachers) against legal restraints on workmen combining in unions, but not because they could thereby raise their wages. The higher artisans, in skilled trades, might succeed in raising wages by combining, and this would probably do little harm to their employers, who would pass on the rise to the consumer in the form of higher prices. But they would harm the rest of the working class, by contracting the numbers the trade could employ and taking capital from other productive enterprises. They would also harm their own skilled trade by making its members narrow-minded and selfish. Strike action should not be forbidden by law, however, for if it were, workers would never find out the real causes of low wages. The market is the instructor:

Experience of strikes has been the best teacher of the

labouring classes on the subject of the relation between wages and the demand and supply of labour: and it is most important that this course of instruction should not be disturbed. (932)

Mill was also against making trade-union membership compulsory:

No severity, necessary to the purpose, is too great to be employed against attempts to compel workmen to join a union, or take part in a strike by threats of violence. Mere moral compulsion, by the expression of opinion, the law ought not to interfere with; it belongs to more enlightened opinion to restrain it, by rectifying the moral sentiments of the people. (933)

On the question whether such unions, though voluntary, might still engage in some industrial malpractice, such as abolition of piecework, or securing equal pay for skilled and unskilled workers, Mill hesitated. In the end he concluded that it was best to leave to the sanction of public opinion acts which, though damaging in themselves, would occasion more trouble and pain if prohibited by law.

By socialism, Mill did not mean a political movement representing the working class, still less one dependent on trade unions. He meant rather the sort of experiments in co-operation which Marx called Utopian, and his experience of them was confined to what he had read of Owenite communities, the writings of the Saint Simonians and early French socialists like Cabet and Fourier. He did not distinguish as clearly as we would want to, between socialism and communism, but he implies that Owenism is communist and the plans of Saint Simon and Fourier socialist. He never envisaged an alliance between the latter and the centralizing plans of Comte. His views were further complicated by changes of mind prompted by political events. The *Principles* was published before the Revolutions of 1848, and Mill treated socialism in the chapter on Property in Book II, and in Book III, Chapter 7, 'On the Probable Futurity of the Labouring Classes' which he tells us was inspired by Harriet Taylor. He recast the first of these chapters, after the Revolutions of 1848 and the *coup d'état* of Napoleon III had given him much more sympathy with French socialists, and the change appears most fully in the third edition of 1852. The chapter on the working classes saw relatively few changes over that period. Finally in 1869 Mill wrote the *Chapters on Socialism*, which he never finished and which appeared after his death. If we consider Mill's views on socialism in three phases, represented by the first edition of the *Principles*, the third edition, and the posthumous *Chapters*, we can begin to understand the strange avowal in the *Autobiography*, where Mill says that he and Harriet were 'much less democrats' than he had been because they 'dreaded the ignorance and especially the selfishness and brutality of the mass' but also that their ideal of improvement 'went far beyond Democracy' and would class them 'decidedly under the general designation of Socialists' (W i 239).

Throughout, Mill's concern is to compare communism or socialism on the one hand and private property on the other, with a view to deciding which is more favourable to energy, individuality, and public spirit. To begin with, his criticisms are mostly adverse to socialism and in line with the early political economists' criticisms of Owen. Socialist communities might be workable in a federal system, but are inconceivable on the scale of a modern State. They might be competitive in their products if only they could hold down population growth. They might manage without offering their members the incentive of private gain, but as they could not make full use of the division of labour their standards of invention and production would be low, and their communal lives dull. So Mill concludes that what is needed is that private property as a system should be improved rather than abolished, and this means enabling every individual to share in its benefits. By 1852 he has changed his mind on some of the disadvantages of communism. Public spirit might, by education, reach the required level. Public opinion could probably check reckless population growth. Men's mental progress could probably solve the problem of apportioning labour efficiently. If the choice were between communism with all its chances and private property with all its injustices, then the former would certainly win. But, says Mill cautiously, neither system has had a fair trial, and the issue will probably be finally decided by the criterion 'which of the two systems is consistent with the greatest amount of liberty and spontaneity'; and he adds a warning that, though private property may be unjust, communism may be intolerant. 'No society in which eccentricity is a matter of reproach, can be in a wholesome state.' We still do not know whether communism will allow the variety of opinions and talents which are 'the mainspring of mental and moral progression' (W ii 209). This note of warning is echoed in the revision of Book III, Chapter 7, where Mill's dislike of the exploitation of one system and his fear of the uniformity threatened by the other impel him towards the syndicalist ideal of associations of workers pooling their own capital. These he hoped would bring about a 'moral revolution', involving

> the healing of the standing feud between capital and labour; the transformation of human life, from a conflict of classes struggling for opposite interests, to a friendly rivalry in the pursuit of a good common to all; the

elevation of the dignity of labour; a new sense of security and independence in the labouring class; and the conversion of each human being's daily occupation into a school of the sympathies and the practical intelligence. (W iii 792)

The spirit is co-operative, but the machinery is competitive; and as we noted before, Mill, like a good schoolmaster, wants to maintain rivalry as a pedagogic device to ensure continuing progress.

Through the successive drafts of the *Principles* Mill assumes that socialism will be characterized by spontaneous choice and peaceful agitation. By the time he wrote the *Chapters on Socialism*, the first International had been founded, and its early congresses had seen the first glimmerings of a revolutionary movement. Mill knew some of the British trade unionists who were among the first delegates, and he thought they talked more sense than their European counterparts. They were moderate, practical, and more interested in peaceful agitation than revolutionary action. The revolutionaries, he thought, were doomed to failure. Their aim of seizing all the land and capital of a country was 'obviously chimerical' and could only plunge mankind back into the state of nature envisaged by Hobbes (W v 748–9). Mill may not have grasped the import of the theories behind the revolutionary movement, but he knew enough of it to feel inclined to qualify the concessions he had made in 1852. That meant tipping the balanced scales of self-interest and public spirit once more in favour of self-interest; in other words, sounding the alarm against the submergence of individuality:

Already in all societies the compression of individuality by the majority is a great and growing evil; it would probably be much greater under Communism, except so far as it might be in the power of individuals to set bounds to it by selecting to belong to a community of persons like-minded with themselves. (W v 746)

The last sentence shows how alien to Mill was the possibility that socialism or communism might override individual choice. He has little idea that he is dealing not with alternative experiments in living but with rival social systems, two giants who would one day divide the globe between them. Reading him is like watching the performance of a referee in a heavyweight boxing contest. Frail and bow-tied and impeccable, he dances about, well clear of the punches, awarding points. In the first round (1848) he declares for private property. In the second (1852) he declares for socialism, but with a warning about keeping to the rules. In the final round (1869) socialism has committed a foul and private property wins on a disqualification. In the end, one feels the whole contest was staged primarily as a test and vindication of *laissez-faire*. Socialism, which Mill persistently conceives as a set of arguments rather than a portentous political force, is useful mainly because it keeps the advocates of free economic relations from too great complacency.

5 Schoolmaster of liberalism

With the completion of the *Principles of Political Economy* the main elements in Mill's mature philosophy were fixed. His writings in the last phase of his life, from his marriage in 1851 to his death in 1873, elaborate themes he had sketched before 1850. Had he written nothing after the *Principles*, he might have been remembered as a solid theorist who after some uncertain forays into politics and literature had buried his youthful radicalism in two heavy works of philosophy and economics in conscious abandonment of any hope of acquiring a political following. In fact, his fame rests very largely on what he wrote in his last years, and the popular idea of him as the 'saint of rationalism', the lonely and ascetic critic of Victorian complacency and convention, derives from *On Liberty* (1859), *Representative Government* (1861), and *The Subjection of Women* (1869). But for these works, it is quite likely that Mill would no longer be read outside the universities. Through them he became a household word. As they are the culmination of the earliest political thinking, we must first ask what makes them stand out from his earlier work.

Two major events helped produce a change of tone to something more urgent and polemical. The first was the French Revolution of 1848 and its aftermath, the short-lived Second Republic. For Mill this was not just a local event in a foreign country. France for him had, since his boyhood visit, been the country of his ideals, where social philosophy was more advanced and its opponents more readily identified than they were in England, where everything was befogged by compromise and goodwill. When Mill uses a phrase like 'the best writers on the Continent' he almost always means French writers. So when the French Revolution broke out in February 1848 he became very excited, predicting that a French republic would have the effect of republicanizing all Europe 'and England itself probably before we die' (W xiii 732). He admired the constitution of the Second Republic and defended it as 'a digest of the elementary doctrines of representative democracy' (W xx 358). While it flourished, he thought little of his own country. 'The whole problem of modern society . . . will be worked out, as I have long thought it would, in France and nowhere else.' And he added, 'As for England, it is dead, vapid, left quite behind by all the questions now rising' (W xiv 32, 34). Louis Napoleon's *coup d'état* in December 1852 was therefore a shock, the more so as it enlisted the peasantry and the mass of the middle classes against the liberal writers and theorists Mill so much admired. Thereafter Napoleon III was for Mill the epitome of wickedness, 'the most dangerous enemy of the future of humanity' (W xv 610). More important, the sort of alliance which he represented, of brutal power, frightened respectability and mass ignorance, had to be held out as a warning to contemporaries. Mill had always disliked the Catholic Church; but now his remarks on the lower classes became sharper and more contemptuous; while the middle classes, reproached in the *Principles* for their heartless hedonism, are henceforth castigated for their mental complacency as well.

The other event was Mill's marriage to Harriet Taylor in April 1851. During their long friendship they had considered they were victims of the institution of marriage. Rumours that they were the objects of gossip only gave them a sense of superiority to the narrow standards of society around them. When John Taylor died in 1849, their own principles did not require them to marry, but they did, preserving their consistency with an enhanced contempt for the insipidity of ordinary society, and making up for the company they missed by saying they were above it. Not that they flouted the canons of respectability. Harriet in particular was deeply sensitive to any hint that her connection with Mill had been improper, and she laid a ban on any she suspected of gossip.

> Tocqueville is a notable specimen of the class which includes such people as the Sterlings Romillys Carlyles Austins—the gentility class—weak in moral [*sic*], narrow in intellect, timid, infinitely conceited, and gossiping. There are very few men in this country who can seem other than more or less respectable puppets to us.

The list, as Mill's biographer notes, included 'almost every man Mill had ever liked'. Mill's upbringing and education had given him an 'instinct of closeness' and an idiom which it had taken him years of effort to turn into a style accessible to a wide readership. His marriage, instead of widening his circle further, probably increased his sense of isolation and confirmed his highly intellectual view of human life. Once he had felt that, while he had the intellect, others had the emotion without which intellect remained ineffective. Now he had both, and the consciousness made him much more complacent about his heritage, and much less receptive to correction from outside.

The extent of Harriet's influence on Mill has been much debated. Some writers treat his claim that some of his later works were their joint productions as literally true. Others, contrasting his magisterial clarity with her breathless, unpunctuated letters have claimed that she merely gave him back his own measured and qualified views in a more opinionated and dogmatic form. Probably a definitive conclusion is not possible. But one effect of her influence is fairly clear. She made him recast his entire conception of social justice. He was led by her feminism to see the major division in society to be not that of the labouring classes and their masters, but simply that of women and men. The dominion of men over women, he came to feel, was the last vestige of 'the system of right founded on might'; women were 'the subject-class . . . in a chronic state of bribery and intimidation combined' (E 434, 439). So the old division of society into the oppressors and oppressed was given a new lease of life and the political imagery of radical agitation revamped to fit the battle of the sexes. Mill recovered a motive for engaging in polemic, this time with the advantage of an established reputation as a philosopher and economist, whose scientific caution was beyond dispute.

Illness gave urgency to what he had to say. Mill had caught tuberculosis from his father and he seems to have given it to his wife. It was a common disease in Victorian England and it was thought to be fatal. Under its threat both showed great courage. The thought that most oppressed them was that they had works still to write which death might cut short. So they planned a series of essays to say what they had to say in a condensed form. If they lived they could add to them, if they died they would serve, as Mill put it (in words which one must remember were written privately to Harriet) as 'a sort of mental pemican which thinkers, when there are any after us, may nourish themselves with & then dilute for other people' (W xiv 141–2). The essays were to be prefaced by 'the Life', or what became the *Autobiography*, in which she wanted him to use his reputation to tell the world the truth about their relationship. In the event, Mill recovered his health with an extraordinary journey through France, Italy, and Greece, while Harriet's condition grew rapidly worse. The essay project was not completed. The only one which they were able to finish jointly before her death in 1858 was *On Liberty*, which Mill published the following year with a dedication to her memory. Their collaboration makes it in tone and manner quite unlike his other works.

These background factors explain *On Liberty*'s desperate urgency of tone. It is much more condensed than most of his works. It compares in style with the finest of the essays of his prime, deploying a complex argument in clear, calm prose, varied by passages of plangent eloquence. It is in itself a striking example of one of Mill's themes, the need to consider the opposing point of view. In fact Mill sometimes sets out objections to his case more eloquently than he puts the case itself, which may account for the fact that his critics often borrow their points from him. But the central principle, that we are justified in interfering with an individual's actions if they are harming others, but not if we merely wish to do him good, is so forcibly and memorably argued that it has passed into the public philosophy of all the great Western democracies.

The long-term influence is not so easy to explain. To anyone coming to the essay from Mill's previous writings, most of its ingredients will be fairly familiar. Its central contention, the 'single truth' of which Mill claimed it was the philosophic textbook, is a sharpened-up version of the political economists' view that certain activities are better left to the individual than the State, and that while the State may and should take the initiative in matters concerning the public good such as defence, public order, and welfare, there is a private area which may and should be left to the operation of self-interest. Adam Smith and Ricardo wanted to protect this area from the State in the name of commercial enterprise: Bentham was more concerned by the threat of religion enlisting the law to interfere in moral freedom. That there must be a private realm which the laws cannot reach was common to all Mill's mentors. His contribution was to try to reduce it to a simple working principle,

> that the sole end for which mankind are warranted, individually or collectively, in interfering with the liberty of action of any of their number, is self-protection . . . The only purpose for which power can be rightfully exercised over any member of a civilized community, against his will, is to prevent harm to others. His own good, either physical or moral, is not a sufficient warrant. (E 14–15)

Mill then makes the famous distinction between self- and other-regarding actions;

> The only part of the conduct of any one, for which he is amenable to society, is that which concerns others. In the part which merely concerns himself, his independence is, of right, absolute. Over himself, over his own body and mind, the individual is sovereign. (E15)

Yet this distinction is sometimes said to be inconsistent with utilitarianism, especially in the light of Mill's disclaimer a little further on, that he does not want to avail himself of any theory of natural rights to defend liberty, but thinks utility is 'the ultimate appeal on all ethical questions' provided it is 'utility in the largest sense, grounded on the permanent interests of man as a progressive being' (E 16). The principle of utility is supposed to measure happiness in units of pleasure and pain, in order to offer an objective justification for interfering in the individual's conception of his own good. A course of action which promotes the general happiness might well have to sacrifice the liberty of the individual for the greater good of the whole. Did not Mill himself think that there should be laws forbidding marriage unless the parties to it showed they had the means to support a family (E 132–3)? Can there be, for the strict utilitarian, any area of private action inaccessible to constraints made in the name of the public happiness?

A similar point can be made from the viewpoint of the individual. It is said that there can be no such thing as a purely self-regarding action, even for a utilitarian. For utilitarianism is a consequentialist theory: the goodness or badness of an action lies in its consequences in pleasure and pain. To say that my misconduct is no concern of yours, though it might give you, and perhaps others too, a lot of distress, is to make an exception to the rule of utility. Mill argues that we should not interfere with a man merely for being drunk, but only if his drunkenness affects others, such as his dependants or his colleagues. But even solitary drunkenness affects others. A pledged teetotaller for instance might experience a physical revulsion equivalent to acute pain on seeing a man drunk, and a whole society which disapproves of alcohol might well enact measures against its consumption to secure the greatest happiness of the greatest number.

But Mill has a utilitarian answer to both these points. By specifying that he appeals to utility 'in the largest sense, grounded on the permanent interests of man as a progressive being' he is evidently appealing to his father's version of the doctrine rather than Bentham's. He specifies three exceptions to his 'very simple principle'. These are minors and invalids, both of whom must have their conduct regulated by others, and (more embarrassingly to modern readers) 'barbarians'. This is Mill the Indian administrator, invoking the cultural ladder of his father's *History*. Some peoples are so backward as not to know what is in their best interests. They represent a stage of

97

development 'in which the race itself may be considered as in its nonage' (E 15). For such people, 'despotism is a legitimate mode of government . . . provided the end be their improvement'. That means they are a proper object of interference on utilitarian grounds. The arguments of *On Liberty* are not for them, but only for people who have reached 'the capacity of being guided to their own improvement by conviction and persuasion' (E 16).

Mill's answer to the second point is also compatible with the principle of utility. It is very fairly set out in Chapter 4. He does not deny that a man's self-regarding actions may give pain to others. But he does deny that such pain always licenses their interfering with him. He does not (as some of his critics suppose) advocate letting an individual 'go to the devil in his own way'. He thinks that society ought to express its displeasure, without going to the length of actual penal sanctions, at foolish or disagreeable conduct, and that the individual citizen's duty to remonstrate with a wrongdoer in such cases is too little recognized or acted upon (E 95). He makes a very careful distinction between behaviour for which the agent is left to suffer the natural consequences such as unpopularity or even ostracism, and acts which so affect the interests of others that society must take a hand in the consequences with actual punishment. To the objection that 'no man is an island', that even minor follies do harm by example, Mill insists that a man may be punished for harming others, but not for harming himself. Should not individuals then be protected from themselves? Mill's reply is, not if they are adults; for more harm is done by interfering than by tolerating the fault. For 'the merely contingent, or, as it may be called, constructive injury which a person causes to society . . . the inconvenience is one which society can afford to bear, for the sake of the greater good of human freedom' (E 100–1). He supports this with two further arguments: that society has in its educational system the means, anterior to the fault, of inculcating rational conduct, and if in spite of this its adult members continue to behave like children, it is itself to blame; and that when society does interfere for the individual's own private good, it will generally make mistakes. Mill then illustrates this last point with examples of societies in which a 'moral police' has enforced a principle which it ought to have left as a matter of private choice or taste. The examples are: the Moslem aversion to pork, the Catholic prohibition of a married priesthood, the temperance legislation in Maine, socialist demands for the equalization of wealth, the temperance agitation in England, sabbatarianism, and finally the Mormon practice of polygamy. Of the last, Mill is careful to expresss his deep disapproval; but he cannot resist a feminist point, that if women are brought up so ignorant as to think marriage 'the one thing needful', it is hardly surprising that some should prefer to be 'one of several wives, to not being a wife at all' (E 113). Throughout this part of the argument his concern is the utilitarian one that one learns morality, at least in part, from the experience of consequences, and that if one is denied that experience by well-meaning busybodies who assume they know what one's best interest is, one will remain morally immature.

Mill's argument for tolerating some morally objectionable behaviour is powerfully reinforced by his case for freedom of thought and discussion, in Chapter 2, the longest in *On Liberty*. Here too one is struck by his fidelity to his heritage, in this case the associationist psychology and the radical empiricism based on it which he set out in the *Logic*. Indeed most of the exaggerations of this chapter stem from this fidelity. Mill's main argument is that we cannot afford to suppress any opinion held by a minority, and he makes the case in three parts. If the received opinion is false and the minority opinion true, suppressing the latter involves an assumption of infallibility which will harm mankind. If the received opinion is true and the minority one false, then the suppression will deprive those who hold the received opinion of the means of knowing why it is true. If, as in the majority of cases, received and minority opinion are each a mixture of true and false, then suppression is an interference with the process of competing opinions by which one generation learns from another's errors. As a plea for fair treatment of minorities and for open-mindedness towards novel opinions, Mill's argument has become part of liberal orthodoxy; but the assumptions behind it have been largely forgotten, and so the most important section of the essay is actually the least discussed.

The guiding conception is the associationist view of the mind. The strength of human judgement depends on 'one property, that it can be set right when it is wrong' (E 27). Why do we trust a man's judgement? Because, Mill replies, he has observed 'the steady habit of correcting and completing his own opinion by collating it with those of others'. He is not merely asking for us to be fair to opinions which differ from ours: he is asserting that there is no other means available to the human mind of attaining truth: 'No wise man ever acquired his wisdom in any mode but this; nor is it in the nature of human intellect to become wise in any other manner' (E 28). There are several things to note about this. The first is that it confuses wisdom and open-mindedness. We often find that people who appreciate every side of a question find it hard to make a final decision, while those on whom we rely for wise, practical advice are not so much open-minded as experienced and without illusions. For Mill the acquisition of wisdom is so cerebral a process, embracing both an appetite for novelty and a suspicion of convention, that his wise man looks a little like a weathercock turning in every intellectual breeze.

He also seems to exaggerate the role of discussion in eliciting truth and keeping it alive. He does not make any clear distinction between polemical debate and temperate discussion. Writing militantly, his mind running on the struggle of rationalism with religious dogma and intolerance, he conveys the impression that only heretics can be discoverers and that those in authority are by definition opposed to new truth. But his choice of heretics is rather confusing. When he asks us to suppose cases where the received opinion is false and the minority opinion true, his examples of the latter are Socrates and Jesus Christ. This makes his argument hard to follow. For while Socrates provides an example of a teacher executed on the false charge of corrupting youth, the case of Jesus is quite different. Mill did not disapprove of Jesus's ethical teachings (which he was later to praise as including 'the ideal perfection of utilitarian morality') but he disliked Christianity, and seems to have shared Gibbon's view that the early experience of persecution taught it intolerance. Mill's case against Marcus Aurelius' persecution of the Christians seems to be, not that it delayed the eventual triumph of Christianity, but that, seeking to suppress it rather than improve it, he ensured that it was a worse religion which triumphed under his successor Constantine. So his examples carry him away from his stated intention. It turns out that he is not telling us what happens when falsehood in authority tries to stamp out truth, but rather illustrating the possibility that authority, though acting in good faith, may yet, by persecuting an opinion it thinks objectionable, make it still worse. Even when he goes on to discuss the case when the received opinion is true and the minority one false, his target is again Christianity, this time as an intolerant creed whose formularies tend to ossify the minds of its adherents, preventing the entry of fresh convictions, yet 'itself doing nothing for the mind or heart, except standing sentinel over them to keep them vacant' (E 51). It was natural that, in spite of Mill's evident admiration for Protestant heretics, many people took this part of his argument as a covert attack on the Christian religion. Under pretence of describing the survival of truth, Mill has actually been castigating the spread of creeds.

When Mill turns to consider open discussion in relation to other sorts of opinion, his strong dislike of dogmas or formularies raises problems. Much popular morality for instance takes the form of well-worn maxims and proverbs. Is a man who directs his actions by such unquestioned principles as 'Thou shalt not steal' or 'Honesty is the best policy' really allowing a part of his mind to go to sleep, or appointing a sentinel over it to keep it vacant? People hold to such principles habitually so as to free their minds and energies for other things: life would be intolerably complex if one had to keep one's most cherished principles under contrast review. In *On Liberty*, Mill partly admits this, though he insists that such maxims would be more valuable if people could hear the arguments for and against before adhering to them. But in *Utilitarianism* he makes his position more clear. The stock case against utilitarian ethics, made by opponents from Burke to Whewell, was that there are relatively few cases of moral decision where the agent has time to make the calculation of consequences. When he came to deal with his objection in *Utilitarianism*, his reply was that there had been 'ample time, namely the whole past duration of the human species' to calculate and weigh the consequences; the results of the calculation were handed down in traditional moral maxims. But even this concession to convention he made reluctantly, calling the maxims so passed on 'the rules of morality for the multitude, and for the philosopher until he has succeeded in finding better' (W x 224). Only the vulgar cling to such maxims and the philosopher alone can leaven the lump of conventional opinion.

Mill's argument for continuous discussion is even more awkward in the case of scientific knowledge, for here he was committed to the eventual achievement of certainty. It may be plausible to say that a particular scientist's solitary researches are really an internal dialogue, in which he argues a case *pro* and *con* with himself. But can it be true that the resulting scientific truths have no better credentials than a 'standing invitation to the whole world to prove them unfounded' (E 28–9)? Mill himself sees that he has come near to saying that truths are useless once they are established and that 'the fruits of conquest perish by the very completeness of the victory' (E 54). His positivism commits him to the view that as men progress in knowledge, the area of possible dissent must contract. But would not mankind in that case have less and less of substance to disagree about and therefore to discuss? Yes, says Mill, and when that happens we shall have to invent matter for dispute; and he praises the Socratic method and even has a good word for the scholastic disputations of the Middle Ages as possible ways of keeping mankind intellectually alert once utopia has been reached. The idea that men may one day run out of matters for discussion is reminiscent of his worry during the mental crisis, that they would one day run out of musical tunes.

Mill then passes to a defence of individuality. 'Society', he says, 'has now fairly got the better of individuality' (E 75). Even men's occupational and regional differences are becoming assimilated:

Comparatively speaking, they now read the same things, listen to the same things, see the same things, go to the same places, have their hopes and fears directed to the same objects, have the same rights and liberties, and the same means of asserting them. (E 90)

The lament sounds so much like a protest against twentieth-century conformity, that one has to remind oneself that Mill was talking about the golden age of private enterprise and *laissez-faire*. Contemporaries did not share his pessimism. Macaulay took the opposite view, that the age was marked by extreme eccentricity, and so Mill was 'crying "Fire" in Noah's Flood', Whether meant as prophecy or description, Mill's claim provokes the question, Why should one suppose that people who see the same things, listen to the same things and visit the same places, should all react to them in the same way? Mill thinks they must, because (as we saw in the argument of the *Logic*) he holds a theory of the mind which leaves little room for the idea of personal identity. If the mind is a mere locus of sensations, then identical sensations will produce an identical mind. It is the different identities of different persons which prevent their assimilation by the same circumstances. Mill was more alarmed than his contemporaries at the prospect of the submergence of individuality because he was a more literal-minded environmentalist than most of them. The idea of 'Chinese stationariness' illustrates the difference. It was a common idea in early Victorian literature, and it usually appears as an argument to illustrate the virtues of free trade. The Chinese had reached the stationary state, in which returns on capital investment were too low to act as an incentive to improvement, and so none of them sought to exploit their great natural resources for more than the needs of the moment. Mill uses this argument in the *Principles* (W ii 167–70) in the usual way, to illustrate the benefits of free trade. He repeats it in *On Liberty* with the brief remark that if the Chinese are ever 'to be farther improved, it must be by foreigners' (E 89). But in 1848 Mill saw many compensations in the stationary state. In 1859 these were submerged in the all-pervasive fear of the despotism of custom. 'Chinese stationariness' is Mill's nightmare version of the stationary state, where custom has killed all originality of thought and behaviour by excluding not just foreign capital but foreign ideas.

To counter the deadening effect of convention and prejudice, Mill calls for more eccentricity, because that would encourage genius, which would in turn leaven the lump of mediocrity. This is sometimes taken as an élitist argument, but one must beware using a word which has since become a term of reproach. Mill used 'élite' (E 478, for example) more freely than a modern democrat would dare, but he would have claimed he was an egalitarian. The fact that he wanted to encourage talent does not mean that he thought all talent innate. He had no way of accounting biologically or physiologically for the emergence of genius. Whenever he speaks of men of outstanding ability, political or intellectual, he treats their occurrence as the result of external stimuli acting on physical and mental energies which would otherwise have remained dormant. But on his own principles, genius cannot result from severe external discipline, and so Calvinism is condemned as dwarfing and cramping the individual. This was not because it repressed 'human nature'. Elsewhere, Mill was concerned to show that the collections of attributes which generally went under that label were the result of social arrangements and not their cause. 'Nearly every respectable attribute of humanity is the result not of instinct, but a victory over instinct' (W x 393). The best specimens of 'human nature' were products of education, being either those who had conquered their instincts, or those who had inherited the benefits of previous conquests.

This is perhaps why Mill combined a daring egalitarianism with the most old-maidish prudery. The mixture is well illustrated in *The Subjection of Women*. In arguing against the legal disabilities under which women then suffered, he refuses to credit any argument based on 'natural' differences between the sexes. 'What is now called the nature of women is an eminently artificial thing—the result of forced repression in some directions, unnatural stimulation in others' (E 450–1). Mill writes as if the position of women were wholly the result of a conspiracy by men bent on keeping them subordinate and ignorant. But when he deals with what he calls 'the sensual relation' he cannot suppress his disgust at the thought of the numbers of women, as he thought, enslaved against their inclinations to men, the vast number of whom 'are little higher than brutes'. It is puritanism rather than snobbery which accounts for Mill's distaste for 'the mass'. Rational behaviour for him necessarily involved a subordination of the passions, and it was the evidence of the pervasiveness of 'the animal instinct' which, more than any other factor, persuaded Mill that rational individuals were a small minority. *On Liberty* is full of phrases like 'those in advance of society in thought and feeling' or 'those who stand on the higher eminences of thought' (E 82). They express Mill's conviction, not so much that talent and ability were in short supply, as that the education and 'self-culture' which produced the 'developed' individual were insufficiently understood and practised. The science of ethology which was to underlie such educaton was unfortunately still to come; meanwhile, the best thing the reformer could do was to hold at bay the erroneous theories whose prejudiced devotees threatened to engulf those on 'the higher eminences of thought'.

Of course Mill valued individuality for its own sake. 'It really is of importance,' he says, 'not only what men do, but also what manner of men they are that do it' (E 73). But he did not want people to be left alone to develop their own nature, partly because he thought there was no such thing, and partly because he could only conceive of development as taking place in conditions of completely free choice. Custom and convention were, by definition, at odds with free choice. 'He who lets the world, or his own portion of it, choose his plan of life for him, has no need of any other faculty than the ape-like one of imitation' (E 73). That meant that the progress of mankind was in the hands of those who had broken free of convention, the developed, the initiators. Everyone should be equally free to choose, but the undeveloped choose only between one custom and another; the developed initiate new behaviour, experiments in living.

The driving impulse behind *On Liberty* is the sense that the available genius in society, which Mill carefully defines as 'originality in thought and action' (E 81), was not enough appreciated or used, and that if the surrounding mediocrity did manage to stifle it, progress would cease. It is a plea for the small thinking minority in contemporary England to be given more air and a wider hearing. Mill complains that

> With us, heretical opinions do not perceptibly gain, or even lose, ground in each decade or generation; they never blaze out far and wide, but continue to smoulder in the narrow circles of thinking and studious persons among whom they originate, without ever lighting up the general affairs of mankind with either a true or a deceptive light. (E 41–2)

The effect was to discourage 'the open, fearless characters, and logical, consistent intellects, who once adorned the thinking world'. Without such intellects, no people could attain 'a generally high scale of mental activity'; but with them, there was hope that 'even persons of the most ordinary intellect' would be 'raised to something of the

107

dignity of thinking beings' (E 44). Mill is not asking that the thinking minority be handed the levers of power to raise the mass to this level. He wants them to do so by teaching and example. He declares,

> No government by a democracy or a numerous aristocracy, either in its political acts or in the opinions, qualities, and tone of mind which it fosters, ever did or could rise above mediocrity, except in so far as the sovereign Many have let themselves be guided (which in their best times they always have done) by the counsels and influence of a more highly gifted and instructed One or Few. (E 82)

But he adds that he is not for hero-worship; all he wants is that the exceptional individual have 'freedom to point out the way', while it is 'the honour and glory of the average man' that he is capable of following 'with his eyes open' (E 82). More explicitly than in the *Principles*, Mill makes clear that his ideal is a pedagogic one, a society organized like a classroom, where the teachers justify their leadership by imparting their knowledge freely, and the pupils give obedience and respect to those who most deserve it, those from whom there is most to learn.

It is a distortion of Mill's argument to suppose that he advocates eccentricity of behaviour, or new 'experiments in living', from a mere dislike of conventional morality and in the name of a free, 'permissive' society. What he advocates, consistently with his vision of an educated minority giving an enlightened lead, is more argument and reasoned remonstrance. He says in Chapter 4 that the office of advising our neighbours about their conduct ought to be 'much more freely rendered than the common notions of politeness at present permit' (E 95). He wanted to see society's morals not merely diversified, but improved.

Conservative critics have seen him as the apostle and forerunner of a modern type, the high-minded liberal who schools himself to tolerate distressing behaviour in his own circle for the sake of unspecified benefits to the species which he will not live to see. But Mill never envisaged the social changes which have produced this failure of moral nerve, and he would certainly not have approved of its effects.

On Liberty, then, may seem to be 'élitist' in the role it gives the thinking minority in society, but this minority owes its position to its own efforts, not to privilege or birth, and retains it in conditions of the freest enquiry. Its function is to educate and improve the mass, but it is given no special aids in this except the knowledge that its leadership depends on its openness and honesty. All this however is more implied than explicitly stated. Mill had still to show how the relationship of reciprocal respect might be made to work. This was the aim of *Considerations on Representative Government* (1861). There the argument of *On Liberty* is translated into what Mill saw as workable political arrangements. To form a just picture of Mill's mature political views the two works must be read together.

In fact they seldom have been. *Representative Government* is twice as long. It contains a wealth of reading and reflection, but diluted into general assertions which seem removed from reality. (In this respect it contrasts with a more popular contemporary work, Bagehot's *English Constitution*, which aims to be purely descriptive, but seems to be so rooted in actual observations of human behaviour that it has worn much better.) Mill's practical proposals too have embarrassed democrats and almost led to the book's being dropped (as *On Liberty* has never been) from the canon of liberal classics: for it advocated proportional representation and plural voting, discarded the secret ballot, and made the suffrage conditional on the literacy of voters. Only the first of these has promised a revival of interest in the book in recent years. But despite its relative unpopularity *Representative Government* amplifies the arguments of *On Liberty*.

The first assumption common to both works is that government cannot be morally neutral; it must improve its subjects or retard them, there was no such thing as simply governing. Those who said that governments were merely to keep order, and spoke of their institutions sometimes as machines to be judged by their efficiency, sometimes as organisms to be reverently left to grow by themselves, were really denying that institutions have an effect on the moral level of those who live under them. In backward states of society men might need to be coerced for their own good, but even paternalistic government must be judged by whether it improves men or keeps them backward. Equally, the institutions of an advanced society never work of their own accord; they too improve or stultify those who live under them. Both the mechanistic and the organicist views of political institutions underrate the power of human agency. 'It is what men think, that determines how they act' (E 156). Even if their thoughts proclaim a backward state, that too is a matter of education and therefore of human agency. So Mill steered between the blueprints of Bentham and the historicism of Comte to conclude that men can, within cultural and historical limits, shape the forms of government under which they live.

But what makes one form better than another? As in *On Liberty*, Mill eschews a theory of natural rights which might offer some universal yardstick. Instead he judges a government by the degree to which it is able to prepare its subjects for promotion to the next rung in the ladder of civilization. Proof of improving intentions legitimizes authority. By this standard the Greeks score higher marks (as one would expect from a classically-educated examiner) than the Chinese. The Greeks turned savage peoples into slaves, but being a Greek's slave was better than being a savage. Whereas the Chinese took their people up to a certain stage, and lacking the intellectual capacity to go further, froze them there. Clearly this is an elaboration of the sentiment we met in *On Liberty* that despotism is a legitimate government for dealing with barbarians. And just as there he dismisses backward peoples and their polities as irrelevant to this theme, so in *Representative Government* he tells us that he cannot deal with the complex questions of which governments suit which states of society, and passes immediately to a description of the ideally best form, which he has no doubt will be one or another variety of republicanism.

His case for representative government is of course that it is the form most calculated to call forth the energies of the largest number of individuals. Despotic or aristocratic governments, however well disposed, encourage passivity and self-regard in their subjects. Popular governments encourage activity, self-confidence and emulation. Mill, it is worth noting, does not follow his father in deriving democracy from the universal tendency in men to oppress one another. He points out that, though the working classes in England are excluded from power, no other 'rulers in history have been actuated by a more sincere desire to do their duty to the poorer portion of their countrymen' (E 188). His own case for popular participation in government is not that governments without it are oppressive, but that it is the best way of ensuring a self-reliant and public-spirited people. His father's concern was with minimizing oppression; his own is with maximizing responsibility.

But then why should not these benefits be extended to backward peoples without delay? Mill's answer, prophetic of the failure of constitutionalism among underdeveloped peoples in this century, is that a people must have reached a level of education and self-reliance before it can use representative institutions. Until it has, despotic or bureaucratic government would be more effective and even more just. Even as he wrote, the Russian autocracy's abolition of serfdom was illustrating his point. But Mill's old radical dislike of an aristocratic parliament comes out in his reasons for his preference. Representative assemblies, he says, reflect more faithfully than unrepresentative governments the faults of their society (E 206). Of course a monarch and his counsellors in a backward society might share its faults, but that is exactly what justifies bureaucratic rule over backward peoples by 'foreigners, belonging to a superior people or a more advanced state of society'. They are equipped to carry their subjects 'rapidly through several stages of progress' and clear away 'obstacles to improvement which might have lasted indefinitely if the subject population had been left unassisted to its native tendencies and chances' (E 207). Mill is obviously thinking of British rule in India.

When he considers advanced societies like his own, Mill shows the effects of two generations of official routine on utilitarian thought. Twenty years before he had criticized Bentham for exhausting 'all the resources of ingenuity in devising means for riveting the yoke of public opinion closer and closer round the necks of all public functionaries' (W x 108). Now he calls for an unhampered administration whose members apply their skills with the minimum of legislative interference. Every branch of public administration has it rules, evolved to meet peculiar problems, which members of the legislature often ignore and undervalue. When legislatures interfere in departmental matters, they represent 'inexperience sitting in judgement on experience, ignorance on knowledge' (E

217). Even when legislatures do contain experts, they are partial and concerned to mislead. Mill resents the way legislation carefully prepared by professionals is ruined because the House of Commons 'will not forgo the precious privilege of tinkering it with their clumsy hands'. Select committees were merely places where 'private crotchets', already once overruled by expert knowledge, get 'a second chance before the tribunal of ignorance'. Mill's solution to this amateurism is a Legislative Commission, embodying 'the element of intelligence', which will prepare bills which parliament, embodying the element of will, might pass or reject, but not amend (E 223). There is no mistaking the note of professional resentment in Mill's account of meddling by a parliament of gentleman amateurs.

But what should parliament's function be? It could not govern, nor administer, nor prepare legislation. Instead, it should check the executive by censure, discussion, and publicity, and be 'at once the nation's Committee of Grievances and its Congress of Opinions'. Its function is to talk, but for its talk to be valuable it must contain 'a fair sample of every grade of intellect among the people which is at all entitled to a voice in public affairs' (E 228). Mill is thus led, by his own high estimate of administrative expertise, to contrive a representative assembly talented enough to be an effective counterpoise. Bureaucratic skill will not by itself ensure good government, for following the professional maxims of officials is open to the same objection made in *On Liberty* to following custom: it encourages mental sloth. Bureaucracies 'perish by the immutability of their maxims' (E 234). (It is worth noting that Mill thought that entry by competitive examination would prevent the home civil service from hardening into a 'Chinese mandarinate'. He seems not to have known that China had had competitive examinations for its civil service for longer than any country in the Western world.)

Clearly administrative expertise must be balanced by popular control. The question Mill then asks is, How popular should this control be? We would not expect him to favour popular majorities, and in fact he applies to them exactly the same objection which he had made to aristocratic minorities in his youth; that they are likely to follow their selfish interests against the general good. So strongly does Mill express his fear of the legislative effects of popular ignorance that one wonders why he does not favour the existing representative system, with its high property qualification for the vote, not to mention the anomalous distribution of seats so unfavourable to the larger cities. In fact he does come near to this. He admits that it is 'roughly true' that the existing representation gives a voice to the opinions that matter, but he adds that this cannot continue if the qualification is lowered and the electorate enlarged (E 250). So it is to meet this threat that he favours the scheme of minority representation first devised by Thomas Hare.

The essence of Hare's scheme was that it sought to represent opinions rather than interests. Mill has a rather laborious chapter (VI) in which he explains his divergence from his teachers, who had always opposed the representation of interests. There are two sorts of interest, Mill tells us; immediate and selfish, or distant and unselfish. The virtuous man follows the latter, and is only liable to be diverted from this by the class or group to which he belongs in society. Separate him from this group and you will enable him to act virtuously. Allow him to vote with others who share his opinions, and he will (if those opinions are worth anything) see them represented in the legislature. At the moment they are not, because he is required to vote in a geographical constituency for a candidate whom he has not himself chosen, and whose views may not even overlap with his own. If he votes with the majority, his own views are submerged in the mass; if with the minority he is effectively disfranchised. But if we have notional constituencies, according to a quota system by which a given number of votes, in whatever district they are cast, ensures the return of one member, then every minority of any significance will have a voice. If moreover a voter is allowed a second preference, votes will not be 'wasted' on a very popular candidate who can easily fill up his quota of votes, but will be, so to speak, saved for another minority representative.

The great advantage of the scheme for Mill was that it would return to parliament exactly those people whose voices in *On Liberty* were in danger of going unheard or undervalued:

> Hundreds of able men of independent thought, who would have no chance whatever of being chosen by the majority of any existing constituency, have by their writings, or their exertions in some field of public usefulness, made themselves known and approved by a few persons in almost every district of the kingdom; and if every vote that would be given for them in every place could be counted for their election, they might be able to complete the number of the quota.

A very pedagogic notion, nothing less than a constituency of readers. 'In no other way', Mill claims, 'would Parliament be so certain of containing the very *élite* of the country' (E 258).

Having sketched the two central elements of his representative system, standing for expertise in legislation and critical intelligence to check and ratify its proposals, Mill adds three further refinements, all of them designed to further the ideal of an alert and vigorous public led by enlightened legislators towards the common good.

The first of these was the suffrage. Mill had been most impressed in Tocqueville's description of American democracy by the educative effects of the vote, which made every American a patriot and 'a person of cultivated intelligence' (E 274). He admitted that their 'highly cultivated' citizens tended to stay out of politics because they were outnumbered by the ignorant majority, with the result that their democracy was a political school 'from which the ablest teachers are excluded' (E 275). But with Hare's scheme that need not recur in Britain. Instead, the ordinary labourers would have their horizons widened by the experience of real political discussion, conducted by the most educated. Ideally, Mill wanted this political education to extend to all, but his fear of ignorance led him to insist that no one should have a vote who could not read or write and do simple arithmetic. He also wanted to exclude those who paid no taxes, and anyone on parish relief. Even those provisions might produce an electorate with 'too low a standard of political intelligence', and so he proposed extra votes for those whose occupations indicated a higher level of instruction. He thought this would be less invidious than a property-franchise. Finally of course he asserts that there is no more reason for excluding women from the suffrage than for excluding people for their height or the colour of their hair (E 290).

Secondly, Mill declared against the ballot. This is not as sharp a break with his heritage as some of his critics imply. James Mill had favoured secret voting, but for a special reason. Seeing how frightened the propertied classes had been before 1830, by the radical pressure for a wider suffrage and shorter parliaments, he had sought to reassure them, by laying most weight on the ballot. He argued that this alone would bring about a moral change in the existing system of representation, because it would at once oblige the candidate to stand on his own merits, and free the elector to express a conscientious preference, free of threats or bribery. The Philosophic Radicals who took this up in parliament always treated the ballot as the most practicable of the various radical reforms of the electoral system, and one which, far from threatening the dominance of the propertied classes, would tend to strengthen it, by freeing it of the suspicion of bribery and corruption. They did not envisage the ballot as a mere adjunct to universal suffrage and shorter parliaments as the Chartists did, and in the event their disagreement with the latter delayed both secret voting and suffrage extension by a generation. By 1859 when he first abjured the ballot, John Mill maintained that the chief abuses which had made it seem desirable no longer existed. The middle classes were in the ascendant, tradesmen were prosperous enough to defy customer-pressure at election times, landlords no longer threatened tenants who voted for their opponents. So the ballot was no longer needed as protection for the elector; indeed it would be a positive hindrance to his function of educating the mass by his example. If elections were to be lessons in political responsibility, voting must be open. Publicity would have the elevating effect upon electors which secrecy was to have had upon his candidates in James Mill's original proposal. 'The bare fact of having to give an account of their conduct, is a powerful inducement to adhere to conduct of which at least some decent account can be given' (E 309). John Mill would not even admit that the ballot would be useful when every man and woman had the vote, because the proposition that the community could have no interest at odds with the general interest (his father's contention) 'will be found on examination to have more sound than meaning in it' (E 311).

Finally Mill condemned the doctrine of pledges, which required a parliamentary candidate of pledge himself to particular policies favoured by his supporters as a condition of his election. This was in fact a position Mill had always held, and it may even have been more in harmony with his later than with his earlier views. Radicals in the 1830s had often demanded pledges from their candidates, and among those who opposed the doctrine with a fine aristocratic disdain was the MP for Westminster, Sir Francis Burdett, who managed to combine vast popularity with a consistent refusal to demean himself by canvassing. When Mill stood as candidate for Westminster in 1865 the constituency had long lost its reputation for turbulence, but he also refused to canvass or give pledges. His reasons were not as aristocratic as Burdett's, but they were hardly less exclusive. 'Superior powers of mind and profound study are of no use, if they do not sometimes lead a person to different conclusions from those which are formed by ordinary powers of mind without study' (E 326). Electors must learn that if they wish to be served in parliament by able men, they must not fetter them with conditions. 'A man of conscience and known ability should insist on full freedom to act as he in his own judgement deems best; and should not consent to serve on any other terms' (E 332). Mill as a candidate never had to face a mob as Burdett had, but in his works he had given some hostages to fortune. At a meeting of non-electors which he had, very reluctantly, consented to address, he was confronted with a placard bearing his own words: 'The lower classes, though mostly habitual liars, are ashamed of lying.' He was asked if he had written them. He replied calmly that he had. The audience rose and cheered.

There are other proposals in *Representative Government*, notably on second chambers and local government, which are of interest, but cannot detain us here. Enough has perhaps been said to show that the book closely follows and illustrates the argument of *On Liberty*. If the political system they both point to is élitist, it is so only in the tautological sense that any educational system comprising teachers and taught is élitist. Mill remained loyal to Bentham's and his father's conviction that politics could be made a science, but he could never consent to its being a recondite study inaccessible to the ordinary man or woman. He shared his father's powerful didacticism and could only reconcile himself to forms of expert guidance if the experts justified their leadership by teaching; and to popular compliance if the people were actively engaged in learning and improving themselves. Reading the two books against the background of Victorian politics one may wonder why Mill, fearing popular majorities and mass mediocrity as he did, was not more willing to acquiesce in a representative system which, as we now see, enjoyed a remarkably high level of political debate, high standards of probity among public men, and a record of earnest philanthropy and reform. A brief explanation, and a tentative one, would be Mill's intellectualism. He could not conceal his contempt for stupidity, but he had no great confidence in contemporary manifestations of intellect. To draw comfort from human stupidity and conservatism like Bagehot, or to exploit them like Disraeli, would have been unthinkable treachery to his own principles of energetic asceticism. But pursuing those principles meant a perpetual war against both the privileged and the poor, or what he now, reviving his father's phrase, called the Few and the Many. The Few must be persuaded to shed any arrangements which would shore up their power or perpetuate their influence beyond their strict deserts. The Many must consent to be placed in situations which would call forth their self-improving energies and help them spurn short-term gratifications. It was an uncomfortable programme which made few converts even in the Liberal party, where its puritanism was likely to have the strongest appeal.

Even in the cause of feminism, where he became something of a leader with a following, his views are a strange blend of abstract deduction and subjective feeling. The *Subjection of Women* was written in Avignon in the winter of 1860–1, and it belongs in mood with the essay *On Liberty*. But Mill did not publish it until events (notably the 73 votes for his amendment to the second Reform Bill proposing votes for women, in May 1867) made him feel opinion was turning his way. It was published in 1869. It is the most passionate and autobiographical of his pamphlets, his final attempt to reconcile utilitarianism with the most romantic experience of his life.

The first half of the essay is an environmentalist polemic against the view that women's legal and political disabilities stem from any kind of natural inferiority to men. Mill denies altogether the force of any arguments from experience, except indeed in the case of vigorous queens, where he claims the evidence is on his side. Men, he holds, have kept women in subjection down the ages, and what they call 'natural' feminine behaviour really means 'customary' (E 440). Until we know more of 'the laws of the influence of circumstances on character' (the unfinished ethology) the common opinions on female nature are merely reflections of male dominance and afford no justification for legal inequalities. Only in conditions of complete freedom of choice will it be possible to discover what each sex is best at doing. Meanwhile, as virtue only derives from experience of consequences, a situation in which only one of the parties enjoys freedom of choice, is morally bad for both. So the family, far from being a refuge of love and trust, is actually an arena for male dominance, a 'school of despotism'. If it is really to be a school of virtue, it must be more like a business partnership, which each party enters with a clear idea of the services owed and the benefits due. But that can never be achieved until women participate on equal terms in the making of the laws under which they live. This part of the argument is purely utilitarian: Mill demands votes for women in exactly the same way as James Mill demanded them for 'the Many', as the only security against oppression by 'the Few'.

When he turns to argue that women are fit for most of the jobs men do, however, Mill reveals a more romantic attitude, perhaps more calculated to have made converts among women themselves. He allows, as 'admitted points of superiority' of women over men, that they are more practical, and have greater nervous susceptibility, greater mental mobility (that is, they can do more things at once) and more intuition. This last Mill carefully defines 'a rapid and correct insight into present fact' (E 494). It is obvious that the 'really superior woman' who possesses these qualities is modelled on Harriet Mill. But she needs a partner. Her intuition cannot be effective until a person whose mind has had the requisite discipline 'takes it in hand, tests it, gives it a scientific or practical form, and fits it into its place among the existing truths of philosophy and science' (E 511). It was an improved version of the partnership of poet and logician which Mill had envisaged in his relations with Carlyle.

But if women have special qualities, should they not have special roles too? Here Mill's romanticism is reined in by his utilitarianism. He warms to the idea of women offering men an ideal to strive for, and he calls medieval chivalry 'the acme of the influence of women's sentiments on the cultivation of mankind' (E 529); but he wants women not only passively to inspire men's activities but to share them. So he argues that it is their exclusion from the benefits of education which has confined them to certain pursuits, and ensured that even in those they do harm. They are fond of philanthropy, for example; but conceive it to consist of religious proselytism and charity. The first generates religious discord; the other mistakes immediate for long-term benefit. A proper education will enable them to use their energies better. Mill's severest censure falls on the way a poorly educated woman married to a well-educated man will drag him down. (Here one is irresistibly reminded of the suppressed passage of the *Autobiography* about his mother.) This is why 'young men of the greatest promise cease to improve as soon as they marry, and, not improving, inevitably degenerate'. The only tolerable marriage is between equals, each enjoying 'the luxury of looking up to the other' and having 'alternately the pleasure of leading and being led in the path of development' (E 540–1). As children are mentioned only in passing as 'hostages to Mrs Grundy', Mill can skirt the whole contentious subject of divorce. For him the main purpose of the dowdy and ascetic partnership, and its sole gratification, is the mental improvement of the parties and of society at large.

Conclusion

Mill has often been treated as the quintessential Victorian liberal, but this is due more to his position in academic syllabuses than to his actual reception by his contemporaries. He was an assiduous and conscientious MP for the short time he was in parliament, but he was never a party man, and indeed political parties play no positive role in his writings. For the aristocratic Whig tradition, which gave liberal politics its constitutional experience and its historical pedigree, he had an inherited antipathy. But having, as he himself said, no religious belief, he was also cut off from the much larger number for whom liberalism chiefly meant membership of one of the many Protestant sects. So among the politicians he was always marked out by what Gladstone called 'the high independent thought of a recluse'.

Even as a political thinker he baffled as many liberals as he converted. No one in the Bentham circle had been more thoroughly imbued with its doctrine and outlook, and despite all the influences, reactionary and romantic, which modified individual doctrines, Mill retained the abstract, schematic cast of mind of his teachers. In fact, while other Philosophic Radicals shed their doctrine and were reconciled with the institutions they had once set out to change, Mill tended as he grew older to return to the aims of Bentham and his father. We find him in the 1860s defending the *History of British India* against the criticisms of its second editor, re-editing his father's work as if it was about to undergo a revival, and in the *Examination of Sir William Hamilton's Philosophy* engaging in a fierce polemic with a man long dead in a way reminiscent of his father's *Fragment on Mackintosh*. Here and there he would differ from his father's views, in general terms and without naming him, but the overall theme is the same in the writings of father and son: that the ideal government would be one of philosophers earnestly engaged in educating and improving their fellow-citizens.

This habit of rehearsing the theoretical debates of his youth gave his treatment of contemporary issues an odd slant which puzzled would-be allies who did not see to what extent he had cast his arguments in the form of a debate with his teachers. At the same time his vision of his youth as a heroic age when 'open, fearless characters, and logical, consistent intellects' had 'adorned the thinking world' (E 42), and his conviction that the society of his middle age was hopelessly timid and mediocre, cut him off from the preoccupations of the younger generation. He does not seem to have realized the importance for that generation of Darwin's *Origin of Species*, which appeared in the same year as *On Liberty* and not only did more than associationism to undermine religious belief, but also had wide implications for international relations. Not surprisingly therefore some of the younger liberals found his idiom strange and his proposals irrelevant. It is significant that the most penetrating critics of his views in his lifetime or shortly after his death, such as Bagehot, Goldwin Smith, J. F. Stephen, or W. S. Jevons, were all liberals.

Yet Mill's reputation survived these attacks, and it is not hard to see why. We may read James Mill's *Essay on Government* now mainly because it was attacked by Macaulay, but we do not read *On Liberty* because it was attacked by J. F. Stephen. The very abstraction which made it hard for Mill's contemporaries to know what line he would take on a particular issue, has helped give him a wider readership since, not merely in Britain but everywhere in the English-speaking world. Few English philosophers have been so accessible to the general reader. There are several reasons for this.

One is that Mill was a very self-conscious writer, for all the abstraction of his subject-matter. His *Autobiography* in its final form is so purged of feeling that it reads like an educational treatise; but his theoretical treatises contain passages which throb with feeling. The reason is that difficult problems in Mill's work are seldom treated as mere matters of technical complexity, but always related to a wider moral or social issue. His supposed eclecticism is really no more than a reflection of the division of labour in academic life, which leads specialists to concentrate on particular aspects and neglect the rest. Recent work has shown pretty conclusively the unity of conception that underlies the whole, and this has reminded us what an individual writer he is. Not everyone will be attracted by the personality, but no one can deny one feature which accounts for Mill's appeal, his fair-mindedness. One lasting effect of that period of 'practical eclecticism' in his twenties was that Mill always practised the advice he gave to Bertrand Russell's father, to try to think of an opponent as a man climbing the hill on the other side. He often puts an opponent's case with such clarity and force as almost to weaken his own reply, and if in some of his later writings one finds a note of dogmatism now and again, that is surely because they date from a period when Mill's social circle was restricted and he was cut off from the intellectual variety on which he flourished and from which so much of his best work stems.

This brings us to the third reason for Mill's wide appeal. He had the intuitive (he would have said acquired) tact of a great teacher, which shows in his extraordinary skill at expounding difficult problems in a lucid and attractive way.

His major works, *A System of Logic* and the *Principles of Political Economy*, though surrounded with an undergrowth of commentary which makes them look impenetrable, are in fact set out in a most inviting manner, like the best introductory courses of lectures. For some reason economists resent the fact that Mill sacrificed originality to the aim of making their subject attractive to generations of students, but the lay reader can have no doubt that this is an advantage. The *Logic* too had an enormous impact, which is best shown by its reception in those two strongholds of clericalism, Oxford and Cambridge. To young men perplexed by the waning authority of the Church on the one hand and the onset of democracy on the other, Mill's own quest for certainty had an obvious appeal. He was, as the legal writer A. V. Dicey put it, 'a teacher created for, and assured of a welcome in, an age of transition'. It was this function as a teacher which gave Mill his influence with the men of letters of the next generation, men like John Morley and Leslie Stephen. It was through them that Benthamic utilitarianism, which began its career as the creed of a small coterie, was brought into the mainstream of English liberalism.

Note on sources

Mill's remark on p. 5 is recorded by Caroline Fox, in H. N. Pym, *Memories of Old Friends* (1882), p. 85. The quotations from Bentham on pp. 6–10 are from *Introduction to the Principles of Morals and Legislation* [1789], edited by J. H. Burns and H. L. A. Hart (London, 1970), pp. 293, 188, and 292 and from *Of Laws in General*, edited by H. L. A. Hart (London, 1970), pp. 235 and 284. Bentham's comment on his prisoners (p. 12) is quoted by J. Dinwiddy in 'The Classical Economists and the Utilitarians' in E. K. Bramsted and K. J. Melhuish (eds), *Western Liberalism: a History in Documents from Locke to Croce* (1978), p. 21. Quotations from Ricardo on pp. 14 and 16 are from Ricardo's *Works*, edited by P. Sraffa (Cambridge 1962–6), viii, p. 184; i, p. 93; and vii, p. 208. James Mill's remark quoted on pp. 23–4 is from the same work, ix, p. 332. Keynes's remark on Ricardo's influence, quoted on p. 18, is from the *General Theory* in *Collected Writings* (1973), vii, pp. 32–3. James Mill's *Essay on Government* and Macaulay's criticism of it, on pp. 22, 28, 63, and 64 are in J. Lively and J. C. Rees (eds), *Utilitarian Logic and Politics: James Mill's 'Essay on Government', Macaulay's Critique and the Ensuing Debate* (Oxford, 1978), pp. 73, 94, 101, 128, and 167. Other quotations from James Mill are: pp. 23 and 25, from the *Essay on Education*, in W. H. Burston (ed.), *James Mill on Education* (Cambridge, 1969), p. 71; pp. 26 and 27, from the *Fragment on Mackintosh* (2nd ed., 1876), pp. 164, 270, and 289–90; p. 37, from my selection of the *History of British India* (Chicago, 1975), p. 190; and

p. 38, from the *Analysis of the Phenomena of the Human Mind* (2nd ed., 2 vols, 1869), ii, p. 213. Coleridge is quoted on pp. 45 and 46 from J. Colmer's edition of *On the Constitution of the Church and State*, Vol. x of the *Collected Works*, edited by K. Coburn (Princeton and London, 1976), pp. 45 and 69. Whewell is quoted on p. 62 from *Philosophy of the Inductive Sciences* (2nd ed., 1847), p. 42. Harriet Mill's remark given on p. 93 is from M. St.J. Packe's *The Life of John Stuart Mill* (London, 1954), p. 338. Dicey's tribute to Mill in the last paragraph of this book is given in C. Harvie, *The Lights of Liberalism: University Liberals and the Challenge of Democracy 1860–86* (London, 1976), p. 40.

Further reading

For the serious student of Mill the great edition of the *Collected Works of John Stuart Mill* now being edited under the general direction of Professor J. M. Robson at Toronto is indispensable. The 21 volumes so far published include all Mill's letters and major works. Two offshoots of the Toronto edition offer as full a guide to writings about Mill as can be found: Michael Laine's *Bibliography of Works on John Stuart Mill* (Toronto, 1982) and the biennial *Mill News Letter*, the former listing everything of importance to 1978, the latter current work. What follows is a selection of work I have found useful.

The best biography of Mill is still M. St.J. Packe's *The Life of John Stuart Mill* (London, 1954), though it is better on the man than his work. A good general study of Mill's thought is J. M. Robson, *The Improvement of Mankind: the Social and Political Thought of John Stuart Mill* (Toronto and London, 1968). Alan Ryan's *J. S. Mill* in the Routledge Author Guides Series (1974) is excellent.

The background to the utilitarian movement is best studied in Élie Halévy's *The Growth of Philosophic Radicalism*, trans. Mary Morris (London, 1928). But Halévy was not strong on the Scottish background on which much recent work has been done. For this *That Noble Science of Politics: a Study in Nineteenth Century Politics* by Stefan Collini, Donald Winch, and John Burrow (Cambridge, 1983) is suggestive and important. Halévy's book hardly deals with the movement after 1815: that is the subject of W. Thomas, *The Philosophical Radicals: Nine Studies in Theory and Practice, 1817–1841* (Oxford, 1979). *The*

129

English Utilitarians and India by Eric Stokes (Oxford, 1959) is a fine study. Bentham's work continues to baffle elucidation and absorb public funds, and there are no introductions to it which are both comprehensive and simple, but J. Steintrager's *Bentham* (London, 1977) is clear and brief, Ross Harrison's of the same title (London, 1983) more difficult. *Bentham and Bureaucracy* by L. J. Hume (Cambridge, 1981) is important. Hostile views of Bentham are G. Himmelfarb's essay in *Victorian Minds* (London, 1968) and Charles F. Bahmueller, *The National Charity Company: Jeremy Bentham's Silent Revolution* (Berkeley and Los Angeles, 1982). Ricardian economics is the subject of a vast literature. I have gained most from J. A. Schumpeter's grand, rambling *History of the Economic Analysis* (London, 1954), supplemented by D. P. O'Brien, *The Classical Economists* (Oxford, 1975). D. Winch's introduction to his selection of J. S. Mill's *Principles of Political Economy* (London, 1970) is excellent. P. Schwartz, *The New Political Economy of J. S. Mill* (London, 1968) is the most comprehensive study to date. Ricardian methodology is well analysed by M. Blaug, *The Methodology of Economics: or how Economists Explain* (Cambridge, 1980).

Mill's reception of romantic poetry is most fully dealt with by F. P. Sharpless, *The Literary Criticism of J. S. Mill* (The Hague, 1967). His debt to the Saint-Simonians is efficiently surveyed in I. W. Mueller, *J. S. Mill and French Thought* (Urbana, 1956). R. K. P. Pankhurst's *The Saint Simonians Carlyle and Mill* (London, 1957) is vivid and entertaining. F. A. Hayek's *The Counter-Revolution of Science: Studies in the Abuse of Reason* (Glencoe, Ill., 1952) is a classic if hostile treatment of Saint-Simon and Comte.

On the origins of Mill's *System of Logic*, Oskar A. Kubitz's *Development of J. S. Mill's System of Logic* (Urbana, 1932) is still of historical interest. On the *Logic*'s relation to recent work, Alan Ryan's *The Philosophy of John Stuart Mill* (1970) is brilliant. A pungently expressed view of Mill's inductivism against current conceptions of scientific method is Sir P. Medawar's in *Pluto's Republic* (Oxford, 1984), pp. 73–135.

On Liberty has been more studied than any of Mill's other works. The closest modern analysis is C. L. Ten's *Mill on Liberty* (Oxford, 1980). John Gray's *Mill on Liberty: a Defence* (London, 1983) is the best discussion to date of the relation of liberty to utilitarianism in Mill's thought. J. F. Stephen's *Liberty, Equality, Fraternity* (1873, repr. with introduction by R. J. White, Cambridge, 1967) is much the most readable attack. More acute but for some reason less well known is W. S. Jevons's series of articles in the *Contemporary Review* for 1877 and 1878, reprinted in *Pure Logic* (1890). Bagehot's *English Constitution* (Oxford, 1928) is acute on Mill's views on the civil service and Hare's scheme. Dennis Thompson's *John Stuart Mill and Representative Government* (Princeton, 1976) is the only full study of the book. On Mill's *Subjection of Women*, I have learned most from Julia Annas's article, 'Mill and the Subjection of Women', in *Philosophy*, vol. 52 (1977), pp. 179–94. Two important collections of articles on Mill are J. B. Schneewind (ed.), *Mill: a Collection of Critical Essays* (London, 1969) and J. M. Robson and M. Laine (eds.), *James and John Stuart Mill: Papers of the Centenary Conference* (Toronto, 1976).

Index